The Pendulum Swings
Transforming School Reform

Bernard Barker

Trentham Books
Stoke on Trent, UK and Sterling, USA

Trentham Books Limited
Westview House   22883 Quicksilver Drive
734 London Road   Sterling
Oakhill   VA 20166-2012
Stoke on Trent   USA
Staffordshire
England ST4 5NP

First published 2010

British Library Cataloguing-in-Publication Data
A catalogue record for this book is available from the British
Library

ISBN: 978 1 85856 468 5

Designed and typeset by Trentham Books Ltd
Printed and bound in Great Britain by 4edge Limited, Hockley

Contents

CONTENTS

Tables

Charts

For
Kate Hoskins, Justine Mercer and Dave Allman

Acknowledgements

This review of school reform in England draws upon a wide range of resources. I travel through time from the late nineteenth century to the first decade of the twenty-first; I report my own research and discuss other people's. I speculate about social, economic and political change; I consider the latest brain science and wonder why some of us succeed when others do not; I reflect on the weakness of the sociological imagination. I reconstruct the early days of the comprehensive movement and remember discredited progressive thinkers and practitioners; I identify with the disadvantaged and revisit their struggles for education. As I endeavour to understand, explain and find alternatives to education's tragic path, I draw upon personal friendships and knowledge, accumulated through 40 years service in English schools and universities.

I owe, therefore, an immense debt of gratitude to the places, people and books that have stimulated and informed me during the fantastic educational journey that lies behind *The Pendulum Swings*; and to the friends and family who have nurtured me as I would wish all our students to be nurtured, in a world that has become less kind and less patient than it should be.

The Pendulum Swings includes research evidence and some argument first presented in journal articles and I should like to thank and acknowledge the editors and publishers who have helped me develop insights about the contradictions at the heart of school reform. Full details of the articles are included in the references (see Barker, B. +date). Ideas and material from Forum (2009c) appear in the Preface; arguments from *Journal of Education Policy* (2008) in Chapters 1, 3 and 6; data from *History of Education Society Bulletin* (2002) in Chapter 3; data and arguments from *School Leadership and Management* (2005), *Cambridge Journal of Education* (2006), *School Effectiveness and School Improvement* (2007) and from *Journal of Educational Administration and History* (2009a) in chapter 5. The St Michael's case study (presented and discussed in chapter 4) has not been reported elsewhere.

I have been fortunate in my colleagues throughout my career. Tom Taylor, Rex and Eileen Tregunna, Jeanne Maynard, Bob Davey and Sylvia West helped me come to terms with being a headteacher; Stephen Draper, Roger Boden, Roger Knight, Chris Jordan and Howard Stevenson have been amazingly imaginative friends and pedagogical collaborators. David Kennedy, Bob Johnson, Ann Holland and Margaret and Rob Gwynne have been generous with their time, assistance and hospitality, and have challenged my thinking about the relationship between leadership and school reform. Andrew Harris never ceases to remind me that our imaginative resources come from English literature and history.

The School of Education at Leicester has been my intellectual home since 1996. Brian Simon and Mel Vlaeminke taught me the importance of education history; Maurice Galton supervised my early adventures with ethnographic fieldwork; Clive Dimmock sponsored my late academic career and showed me how to teach post-graduate research students. Bob Burgess happens to be a pioneer of single school case studies, so his encouragement has been invaluable.

Finally, I express heartfelt thanks to Gillian Klein, who suggested the idea of the book, and my lovely daughter Irena, who thought of the title. Kate Hoskins, Justine Mercer and Dave Allman, to whom The Pendulum Swings is dedicated, have accompanied me on the journey. They have eased the loneliness of the long distance writer and have read and commented in detail on the draft manuscript. The mistakes, of course, are my own. My wife Ann does not approve of my hours in front of the computer but she has been my best friend and greatest source of strength for 43 years and I should have written nothing without her unselfish devotion.

Bernard Barker
Peterborough 2010

Abbreviations

A	Advanced Level
ASCL	Association of School and College Leaders
CSE	Certificate of Secondary Education
DCSF	Department for Children, Schools and Families
DfEE	Department for Education and Employment
DfES	Department for Education and Skills
FSM	Free School Meals
GCE	General Certificate of Education
GCSE	General Certificate of Secondary Education
GMS	Grant Maintained School
GNVQ	General National Vocational Qualification
H2, H3	Head Teachers at The Felix Holt School
HMCI	Her Majesty's Chief Inspector
HMI	Her Majesty's Inspector
IQEA	Improving the Quality of Education for All
LA	Local Authority
LftM	Leading from the Middle
LMS	Local Management of Schools
LPSH	Leadership Programme for Serving Heads
MP	Member of Parliament
NCSL	National College of School Leadership; since 2009, National College for Leadership of Schools and Children's Services
NFER	National Foundation for Educational Research
NPM	New Public Management
NPQH	National Professional Qualification for Headship
O	Ordinary Level
OECD	Organisation for Economic Cooperation and Development

Ofsted	Office for Standards in Education
ONS	Office of National Statistics
PAG	Parents Action Group (Hillside School)
PE	Physical Education
PISA	Programme for International Student Assessment
PwC	PricewaterhouseCoopers
QCA	Qualifications and Curriculum Authority
SEU	Standards and Effectiveness Unit
TDA	Training and Development Agency for Schools
TTA	Teacher Training Agency
UK	United Kingdom
US	United States

Foreword

One of the fears I have for education studies is that its history becomes forgotten or simply gets placed in the margins of what we know about schools and schooling. For instance, in the current form of teacher education, there is no place for understanding how the past influences contemporary provision. There is little time or space in many current Master's level courses for how the policies and practices of the past become revisited, 'reinvented and reintroduced' to be looked at.

In *The Pendulum Swings: Transforming School Reform*, Bernard Barker's argument is that the nineteenth century rhetoric of 'payment by results' has been recast and reworked in contemporary education policy. He argues that 'a strong emphasis on hyper-accountability has left no space for alternative, qualitative measures of social care and progress. The relentless pursuit of results has obliterated other concerns'. Yet this is not just a book about the history of education policy making, although this matter is explored. Rather, it is a book about how policy-making might be envisaged in the future.

Bernard Barker's book is rooted in a political and policy-oriented context. Its arguments, that forensically detail the ways in which much of what passes for educational reform does not achieve its intentions, are located in a wide and scholarly set of research findings and evidence that supports his case. His argument that 'deep, historically rooted social and cultural variables influence our chances of success and seem beyond the reach of attempts to fine-tune classrooms and teaching methods' is explored in chapters that ask some enduring educational policy questions such as 'must the disadvantaged fail?' This book is particularly good at teasing out and deconstructing aspects of the educational lexicon such as 'best practice' and 'leadership and modernisation' in order to interrupt and disrupt their normalising tendencies.

The style of the book is original and inclusive and opens out complex issues to immediate understanding. *The Pendulum Swings: Transforming School Reform* makes extensive use of examples of practice in schools and puts forward a strong case for doing schools differently. Bernard draws on his considerable experience of working in education (teaching, leading as a school principal, professor of education) as well as his roots in activism and 'real' school improvement. For example, his case study on implementing the Academy programme powerfully demonstrates the contestations and the complexities that take place at a local level, but that are not widely circulated (except by groups like the Anti-Academy Alliance).

The book draws on wide-ranging cases, research, local struggles and policy research. Bernard claims that 'schools have been taught to chase shadows and dreams, and as a result have neglected the art of the possible'. Through the stories and narratives he places throughout the book, we are helped to see what could be made a reality in our schools.

This is very much a teachers' book, written by someone with a deep-rooted understanding of education policy and the complexities involved in reform. In talking of the promise of progressive principles, Bernard does not hark back to some golden age that needs to be recovered. What he does do is show how a continual cycle of media attention to weakness and failure in schools produces, time and again, 'yet another forlorn initiative'. Instead, what is needed, he believes, is a renewal of 'mutual relationships' where schools and teachers really can make a difference. 'By over-emphasising a particularly narrow set of policy objectives,' he observes, 'government agencies have made themselves a serious obstacle to progress and improvement'.

I started this foreword with some of my fears for the future of education studies. I want to finish with hope. I hope that many of us who work in education, as teachers, tutors, policy-makers, and students of education more widely, read this excellent and highly imaginative book. Bernard finishes this volume with a set of ideas for transforming school reform. This is a book of commitment to a better future and a book, ultimately, of hope.

The book is, moreover, a comprehensive account of the relationship between policy-making and practice. Perhaps more importantly, it is a deeply moral account that helps us understand why we are where we are – and what we could do about it. As the pendulum swings, yet again, let us hope that there can be a move towards the policy recommendations Bernard makes; to take social context seriously; support community coherence and, most importantly, 'increase the emphasis on worth and personal growth'.

Meg Maguire
Professor of Sociology of Education.
King's College London

Preface
Getting the Boys to Sing

Payment by Results

The phrase 'payment by results' is now remembered as a short-hand expression for a distant and dismal period when education for ordinary girls and boys was barely funded at all. It conjures up a picture of a dark-suited Dickensian inspector listening as anxious urchins read or recite their tables, and we give thanks that history is another country. Unfortunately, the payment by results system has been revived in our own time so that another generation of children has grown up under an oppressive regime based on regular tests and cash rewards for 'achievement'.

Discontent with this modern version of learning by rote, testing and inspection has gained strength as the prospect of political change has increased, offering an unexpected opportunity for us to emulate those Victorians who ceased to believe in gloomy inspectors and a dreary basic curriculum. *The Pendulum Swings* analyses the fundamental assumptions that have driven our late twentieth century version of payment by results; considers why there has been so little progress towards the government's goal of social transformation; and recommends an alternative approach to school reform.

Five illusory beliefs have driven education policy:

1. *Effective and efficient schools overcome disadvantage and improve life chances.*

2. *Markets and competition improve school efficiency and outcomes.*

3. *Central regulation and inspection ensure high standards of quality and performance.*

4. *Successful leaders transform their schools and change the system.*

5. *Best practice in teaching and organisation can be transferred from one site to another so that every school performs at a high level.*

The Pendulum Swings investigates the sustained appeal of these false propositions, explores the hopes and fears that may influence the future, and draws upon progressive insights to recommend four strategic priorities for change.

The Revised Code

In March 1862, Matthew Arnold, son of the famous headmaster of Rugby School, Dr Thomas Arnold[1], and one of Her Majesty's Inspectors of Schools (HMI), wrote a scathing attack on the proposal that schools should be funded according to their pupils' results. Arnold criticised the idea that an annual examination of individual children in the three Rs (reading, writing and arithmetic) should decide whether a school received state funding or not. He believed the proposed system of payment by results would turn 'the inspectors into a set of registering clerks', concerned with a mass of minute details about basic English and arithmetic, rather than with judging a school's success in educating children to be citizens of a more truly human society. Arnold condemned the 'religion of inequality' that he found everywhere in England, and insisted that social equality was necessary for the growth of human personality, and for the creation of an enlightened society (Arnold, 1960; Connell, 2002:277).

The Revised Code was introduced and developed nevertheless, so that for over thirty years the children of the labouring classes were subjected to 'the mechanical teaching of the rudiments of literacy', while Arnold's plea for the study of literature in elementary schools was ignored (Connell, 2002:277). After the publication of Arnold's (2006) *Culture and Anarchy* in 1869, however, he became the prophet of a quite different conception of mass education, based on the diffusion of culture and learning through every level of society. He believed school education should be valued according to its success in creating the desire for continued personal growth and contributing to the progressive elevation of society.

By 1895, the Revised Code, designed to reduce the cost of educating the labouring classes, was finally discredited and abandoned. The pendulum had swung decisively against the narrow-minded, mean-spirited class bias of the mid-Victorian period, and Matthew Arnold became an important influence on a new generation of educators who were ready to believe that a liberal education should be the foundation of a better society. Central and local government formed an uneasy partnership during the first half of the twentieth century, with heads and teachers, who became steadily more professional and unionised, taking growing responsibility for their schools and classrooms.

Return to the Past

Since 1988, policy-makers, influenced by global trends and anxieties about economic competitiveness, have reinvented and reintroduced the principal ingredients of the payment by results system. Schools are regularly visited by inspectors who tabulate 'a mass of minute details' to assess student performance, especially in the three Rs, known today as 'the basics' (Arnold, 1960). Teachers are held accountable for test and examination outcomes by at least twenty different mechanisms, so that 'results have become the be-all and end-all for schools' (Mansell, 2007:4). The curriculum has been narrowed so that children are taught only the essentials needed to pass tests. A strong emphasis on hyper-accountability has left no space for alternative, qualitative measures of social care and progress. The relentless pursuit of results has obliterated other concerns, especially those derived from Matthew Arnold's conception of liberal education.

After twenty years of obsessive and unyielding school reform, there are signs that the pendulum is swinging once more against narrow, results-driven conceptions of education. Policy-makers are worried as the evidence accumulates that student outcomes have not improved as much as they were expected to do (Barber, 2008). Parental choice and competition between schools have produced a highly differentiated and increasingly polarised system rather than better grades for all (Levačić and Woods, 2002a). David Hopkins (2007:22), former Chief Advisor of

School Standards, agrees that recent reforms have failed 'to accelerate student achievement in line with policy objectives' and argues that new methods, including teacher leadership and personalised learning, are needed if further progress is to be achieved. Government agencies themselves have begun to argue against the one-size fits all mass production system that has prevailed since 1988, with the National College for School Leadership (NCSL, 2009), for example, eager to promote personalising learning as a 'process which empowers the learner to decide what, where, when and how they learn'.

The *Cambridge Primary Review* (2009) reports an independent three-year study of primary education and concludes that children's lives are impoverished by a narrow, test-driven education that is fundamentally deficient. Sir Ken Robinson claims that the results-driven apparatus is crushing children's expressiveness and creativity. Singing, music, dance, drama and poetry have become optional extras, marginalised by an all-consuming preoccupation with core subjects and achievements that can be measured in numerical terms (Shepherd, 2009). Members of the Labour-controlled House of Commons Children, Schools and Families Committee (2008) agree with this judgement. They believe children in England are tested too much and too often, and that many schools are teaching to the test and narrowing the curriculum to maximise performance.

The difficulty today is that the main political parties, and most of the policy experts who cluster around them, continue to believe in the propositions on which the performance regime is based. Ministers and officials are confirmed in their faith by an international consensus that schools can be made more efficient and effective. The Organisation for Economic Cooperation and Development (OECD), for example, plays an important role in promoting test-based approaches to education that are very similar to those adopted by the UK government (Grek, 2009). Politicians are also uncomfortably aware, however, that we have reached the end of what can be achieved by current methods. They are puzzled by data that shows little change in young people's attitudes, skills and social mobility, despite a huge increase in educational expenditure and opportunity, and sense the swing of the pendulum against command and control methods.

Unfortunately, apart from subtle changes of language that imply greater scope for school and teacher initiative, the government has no idea what to do next. Bureaucratic minds are stuck in the simple world of payment by results, where sticks and carrots are supposed to yield better outcomes. They find it hard to imagine different but more rewarding policy goals, and do not understand how to bring about an environment that is more conducive to a real transformation in the quality of learning and teaching.

Beyond official circles, however, the economic meltdown seems to have produced an intellectual sea change comparable to the late Victorian swing against the Revised Code. Phillip Blond, director of the Progressive Conservatism Project at the think tank Demos, believes we are 'in the middle of a paradigm shift' and are witnessing 'the end of the neo-liberal project' (Derbyshire, 2009:1). Support from the Conservative leadership for his anti-Thatcherite 'Red Tory' views has encouraged him to launch a new think tank, ResPublica, to explore radical ideas based on communitarian civic conservatism. Blond argues that neo-liberal policies have produced a harmful mix of state authoritarianism and atomised individualism. Conservatives, he suggests, should find ways to rebuild communities ravaged by market forces that have paid no attention to local needs and interests (McSmith, 2009; Blond, 2009).

Is There Another Way?
The four part BBC series, *The Choir*, first shown in 2007, demonstrates beyond doubt that there is an alternative, very demanding approach to school improvement, and it provides a glimpse of the changed conditions needed to give schools a realistic opportunity to transform lives and communities. A gifted choirmaster proves that disadvantage is not an inescapable obstacle to a better life (Barker, 2009c).

The BBC chose a boys' school in an inner city area of a relatively deprived Midlands town in England. There has been no tradition of singing or choral work there for 40 years. Teachers and children see singing as for girls and gays; but in reality even these unfortunates have no opportunity to sing. Amongst the school's students are choristers from the Cathedral Choir, who keep very quiet for fear of bullying; and ethnically diverse street rappers who entertain one another in the playground. The programme tells the human story of what happens when these children and their parents meet Gareth, a very young-looking but nationally distinguished choirmaster.

Getting the Boys to Sing

Through a series of four programmes that reflect Gareth's nine months working at the school, with the declared intention of producing a 100 strong choir to sing at the Albert Hall in London, the BBC portrays an astonishing process of school improvement that achieves seemingly magical results.

The Lancaster School in Leicester is long established and has a reputation for sporting excellence. Music is a low profile option after age 13 and there is no singing beyond music lessons. Gareth arrives and discovers strongly negative attitudes amongst the boys and many of their teachers – there is no way the students will sing in front of others, and they tell him he is wasting his time. His first efforts lead to anger and frustration when people are difficult, including the macho Physical Education (PE) teacher who is head of year 10.

Over nine months, the choirmaster devotes his entire time and attention to changing these attitudes and creating a choir of 100 boys. He walks the playground, scouting the terrain and understanding the boys' perspectives. He starts lunch and after school clubs, he finds the boys who have been keeping quiet about their music. He offers individual lessons to promising students, including one of the rappers, who is at first interested, then rejects Gareth in a cloud of anger. As the fledgling choir follows a patchwork path, Gareth takes them to another comprehensive, in a prosperous middle class area, where there is already a tradition of singing and wonderful music. He organises a coach trip to King's College Chapel in Cambridge, where the choir members sing with the choristers. They are excited and awed by their expanding horizons.

Gareth organises a rapper workshop with visiting musicians and wins over the PE department by starting a staff choir that sings on sports day. All the time he struggles to find enough boys and to achieve consistent attendance and commitment. Participants and parents are amazed and as they grow in self-confidence and pride become advocates for Gareth's message that singing is life enhancing and life transforming.

There is a school concert and parents are moved to tears by the first version of the choir. But it isn't big enough – how can Gareth achieve his target of one hundred boys? He takes his devotees to the local primary schools and engages boys who will transfer to Lancaster over the summer. These newcomers boost numbers in the autumn.

We see Gareth working with individual boys, investing hours in teaching them skills and giving them confidence in themselves. Many are from ethnic minorities and this is the first time they have achieved public recognition and success. He struggles with the ensemble, by turns frustrated, depressed and inspiring. Always positive, he keeps the focus on the public performance at the Albert Hall, at first a distant goal but then a looming, terrifying prospect. Eventually he has his choir of 100 and they sing with England's best at the Royal Albert Hall, to the great pride and joy of their parents, teachers and peers. Sport is no longer the only viable option for students at Lancaster.

Towards the end of his residence, Gareth and the choir intrigue to gain meetings with the head (who has seen the whole project as a tremendous boost for the school and students) and governors. How can they ensure that this new tradition does not disappear when the choirmaster leaves?

What did Gareth do?

Gareth's work at Lancaster exemplifies a passionately personal and social approach to improvement that contrasts with the test-driven techniques endorsed by policy-makers and reformers. The choirmaster's apparently intuitive, craftsman-like methods suggest the principles that should be applied to 'make a difference' in the sense of enriching the lives of the students. What did Gareth do?

- He adopted an incremental, pluralistic theory of change. He investigates, interrogates, challenges and demands – he never assumes. He does not believe there is one right answer, a formula for success – he is prepared to try anything and everything. Each student is different and demands time and energy as well as understanding.

- He recognises that you cannot work on one change dimension at a time. All the ingredients – families, students, teachers, school expectations, opportunities to succeed, the music curriculum, the elements of singing, motivation, attitudes, relationships – have to be worked with all at once, in parallel and in series, never in isolation. Collaboration and cooperation are at the heart of Gareth's approach.

■ He never loses faith and belief in himself, in the school, in the boys themselves – he constantly reminds people of their transcending, tangible goal, 100 boys singing at the Royal Albert Hall, and promotes subsidiary objectives (improving skills and motivation, developing confidence and the desire for success) that are genuinely *transformational* and apparently impossible.

■ He works with reality and adopts practical solutions – he is intensely hands-on, engaged and emotionally committed. If the project fails, he fails. He believes in singing so much that he is prepared to risk humiliation on national television. At times he nearly is humiliated, when a student walks out and when seats are empty at choir practice. There is only one test, not a battery of them (at the Albert Hall) – but everyone shares the experience and no one can fail on his or her own. This is a world away from a government singing initiative, with a coordinator appointed, a folder issued, a CD distributed and the inspection manual amended.

■ His choice of outcome (so different from the current obsession with numerical data) is qualitative – a unique, memorable experience that has the potential to change the boys' attitudes, skills, lives. The early, declared outcome shapes the project – this is not a game for elite, gifted individuals (though there are solos, often from unlikely boys) but a corporate endeavour for 100 students where everyone contributes to everyone else's success and no one is left behind. The boys have ceased to believe that singing is not for people like them. Everyone is enjoying success that seemed beyond their grasp.

A Climate for Learning

Gareth's nine months at Lancaster Boys do not provide the groundwork for a straightforward formula that can be rolled out across the country. Gareth's way is too slow, too individual, too particular and too hard to measure. His singing initiative shows that educational problems are deeply rooted in our culture and society, and that their solution depends on investments of skill, commitment and time that are unattractive for politicians and policy-wonks in search of quick, eye-catching fixes. The quick fix is the real substance of reform because it is perfectly adapted to politicians and their constantly changing, short-term imperatives.

Gareth's story helps us understand why government initiatives rarely succeed. It illustrates how the best teachers have always worked and shows the sheer complexity of engineering lasting change in assumptions, practices and opportunity. There are no short cuts, no silver bullets. The lesson of the choir is that the impossible can be achieved, against all expectations, provided we have gifted, passionate teachers who change children's lives by timely and appropriate interventions. There is no alternative to their hard work and there is no substitute for their talent and emotional commitment.

The tragedy of school reform is that teachers with the passion to emulate Gareth's achievements find the climate created by government agencies less than conducive for creative projects. Despite the rhetoric of the 2008 version of the National Curriculum, the regulatory apparatus ensures compliance and discourages initiative, while monitoring, audit and self-evaluation absorb energy once freely given to clubs, societies and other extra-curricular activity. The Lancaster Boys' Choir is an example of the diverse learning opportunities that are squeezed into the margins of school life by necessity because they do not count in the performance tables. The music teacher may get the boys to sing but s/he is rewarded only for getting the General Certificate of Secondary Education (GCSE) results up. She may have produced the musical *West Side Story* but Office for Standards in Education (Ofsted) inspectors are more interested in an upward trend in her value added data. Is it wise to work so hard for uncertain benefits?

In many ways, therefore, the government's performance regime has worked to constrain and even undermine teachers who strive to improve their schools. By over-emphasising a particularly narrow set of policy objectives, government agencies have made themselves a serious obstacle to progress and improvement. The chapters that follow investigate and challenge the policy assumptions that have dominated education for twenty years and consider the changes needed to create positive conditions for teachers who aim, like Gareth, to transform children's lives.

1
Introduction – The Dynamics of School Reform

Shock and Awe

When the 1988 Education Reform Bill became law, I was principal of a large community comprehensive and was quick to mock 'the foolish hope that the Department of Education can transform educational standards and economic performance by setting all the lessons itself' (Barker, 1988). I grimaced when the Secretary of State told the Conservative Party conference that he would not 'tolerate a moment longer the smug complacency of too many educationists, which has left our national educational performance limping along behind that of our industrial competitors' (Baker, quoted in Simon, 1991: 540). Although I understood that we were caught up in an international phenomenon, with politicians 'from Bali to Baltimore ... setting tests, prescribing curricula and blaming the young for falling behind in a global mental arithmetic contest', I under-estimated the relentless, energetic wave of school reform that was inaugurated by the 1988 Act (Barker, 1989:481). It has lasted for 20 years and the shock and awe effect continues to pervade every aspect of education.

As the 1988 Reforms took hold, with a prescribed curriculum, devolved budgets and marketplace competition, I began to experience at first hand the managerial pressures that gradually but inexorably squeezed the space for independent thought and teacher professionalism. Since 1999, I have been an academic spectator, amazed that teachers have found ways to survive and flourish, despite the ferocious accountability regime to which they have been subjected. This book is intended as a tribute to inspired practitioners who have been true to themselves, creating fine experiences for students in the most unpromising circumstances.

My intention is not to complain that education is worse or less worthy than in the past, or that all is in vain, but to argue against a school effectiveness regime that has ground many teachers into the dust, and multiplies the very failures it is supposed to cure. The apparatus has forced schools to work against the policy grain and obliges teachers to discount their professional instincts in favour of glossy recipes from government strategies. The price has been high in terms of lost opportunities and the nervous tension that has eroded the will of so many vulnerable students and teachers. As the pendulum swings, we have to find a better way to improve our schools and support our children.

Improving Education

During the Blair years (1997-2007), the centralising, modernising agenda became almost irresistible as New Labour ministers worked to align public institutions and services with the requirements of the global economy. School reform was the flagship programme, designed to ensure that every child's talents and skills were increased and mobilised as part of a remorseless drive to improve national efficiency and competitiveness. Substantial confidence in the future of public services was generated by a quantum increase in investment.

As John Dunford, general secretary of the Association of School and College Leaders (ASCL), looked forward to Gordon Brown's premiership, he found much to celebrate. A spirit of optimism about what all children can achieve had been engendered, with everyone's worth and potential recognised, regardless of class, ability, gender and ethnicity. A long tail of disadvantaged, disaffected young people lacking basic skills was no longer acceptable. Increased investment had produced schools and colleges better built and resourced than before, while Ofsted reports were encouraging about the quality of leadership and teaching at primary and secondary schools (Dunford, 2007).

By 2007 there was significant evidence that seemed to confirm the success of school reform. Participation rates at every level of education (from nursery to university) had improved considerably and the percentage of students achieving at expected levels had increased proportionately. Between 1990 and 2008, the percentage of pupils achieving five or more GCSE grades A* to C or equivalent in England increased by over 90 per cent (Department for Children, Schools and Families (DCSF), 2008). Universities had expanded to the point where they occupied a strategic place in the economy and society, providing a constantly renewed source of ideas and energy. To everyone's surprise, research by PricewaterhouseCoopers (PwC) found no erosion of the graduate premium as the supply of graduates increased (Universities UK, 2007; PwC, 2007).

Lord Adonis, a Blairite education minister, celebrated the advanced professionalism of a new generation of well-qualified teachers, inducted into the classroom through a rigorous training regime, inspected by Ofsted. After 1998 there was a 54 per cent increase in recruitment to teaching from the Russell Group universities. The Training and Development Agency for Schools (TDA) and the NCSL provided funds and sustained support for teacher education, based on progression through a variety of career paths. Programmes like the National Professional Qualification for Headship (NPQH) and Leading from the Middle (LftM) engaged participants in self-evaluation, reflection and development activities (Adonis, 2005).

End of an Era

Two years later, these perceptions seem to belong to a vanished age. An era of unparalleled prosperity has ended but we have yet to accommodate the long consequences of its demise. The failure of Lehman Brothers[2], on 15th September 2008, signalled an abrupt end to sixteen years of growth, wealth and public investment. As we contemplate the emptying towers of Canary Wharf, the downward swing of the political pendulum can be heard hissing above, poised to scythe through everyone's hopes and expectations. Bankers may be clearing their desks and mourning the bonus years but soon tumbrils will arrive for politicians and policies that cannot adapt to changed conditions.

Meanwhile, nervous observers survey the privately financed schools and hospitals built in English towns and cities during the great age of credit and are reminded of Ozymandias, King of Kings. Shelley describes the ancient monarch's once mighty statue, a massive monument to his imperial grandeur reduced to shards of stone and scattered in the desert sun: 'Nothing beside remains. Round the decay/Of that colossal wreck, boundless and bare/The lone and level sands stretch far way'. The wreckage left by the credit crunch is likely to haunt us for years to come, obliging politicians and everyone else concerned with policy and delivery to come to terms with reduced public spending, lost hopes and an increasingly pessimistic outlook.

This book is about schools and education in England, protected for the moment by the government's decision to keep spending through the worst of the crisis, but ultimately threatened by a potentially devastating combination of changes in climate, resources and belief. The impact of the swinging pendulum is likely to be more profound in education than elsewhere because, for more than twenty years, policy-makers have been blinded by a set of five seductive illusions that have informed some of the least successful government schemes in British history. Labour's education reforms have begun to unravel.

The Pendulum Swings aims to expose the reality behind these illusions, to dissect the policy imperatives that have led to the current crisis, and to demonstrate that there are constructive alternatives, provided our politicians are courageous enough to act on their growing instinct that teachers and children should drive improvement, and that freedom from bureaucratic control is the essential precondition for good education (Gove, 2009). The NCSL's current emphasis on personalised learning, and on student participation in school improvement, needs to inform a new approach, rather than offer an ironic commentary on the command and control culture that pervades and dominates education (Watt, 2008).

Five Illusions
Since 1988 governments have based school reform policy on five distinct but closely related propositions that have proved illusory. Each of these is introduced below and reviewed critically in chapters 2-6.

1. Effective and efficient schools overcome disadvantage and improve life chances

Market pressures, regulation and leadership are believed to encourage schools to adopt best practice and become more efficient and effective. Policy makers are convinced that improved skills and knowledge must overcome disadvantage and stimulate social change and mobility. For Tony Blair, speaking at the Labour Party Conference in 1999, education was an important part of a wider crusade against poverty:

> The frustration, the urgency, the anger at the waste of lives unfulfilled, hopes never achieved, dreams never realised. And whilst there is one child still in poverty in Britain today, one pensioner in poverty, one person denied their chance in life, there is one Prime Minister and One Party that will have no rest, no vanity in achievement, no sense of mission completed until they too are set free. (quoted in Wilson, 2009:352)

Unfortunately, the available evidence on inequality and disadvantage suggests that school reform has failed, even as part of a wider policy regime designed to overcome poverty and improve life chances. Singly and in combination, the reform propositions have not produced the desired results. Diane Reay, Professor of Education at Cambridge University, believes the 'biggest influence on educational achievement is family background' and argues that 'bigger income differences make the social structure more rigid and decrease opportunities for social mobility' (Reay and de Waal, 2009:42). The problem is that students and families are not passive material for school processing, but active participants who are helped or hindered by their material and cultural resources, and have a strong positive or negative impact on their own levels of achievement. The supposedly positive characteristics of particular schools seem to exert no more than a marginal influence on student outcomes, especially if these are measured in terms of test and examination results.

Every indicator shows that social inequality has increased very markedly during the last twenty years and that schools have made no obvious impression on the differential performance of advantaged and less advantaged students. Better examination results have not generated better employment opportunities and improved status for less well off people. Social mobility has declined, with every profession and elite occupation dominated by those who began life as members of families in the top income decile (Milburn, 2009).

Although social inclusion and to some extent social justice have been important priorities for the Blair and Brown governments, the educational effects of relative deprivation remain marked. Children's futures are predictable, with a father's occupation and a mother's education providing important indicators of likely outcomes and prospects. Social geography and inequality exert a continuing influence on success (Clark, 2009; Haque and Bell, 2001). The distribution and concentration of poverty within and between particular neighbourhoods have an important influence on local schools and their relative success, with children more than likely to transmit their disadvantage to the institutions they attend. Social variables seem to trump our best efforts to secure improvement.

2. Markets and competition improve school efficiency and outcomes

Markets seem to have produced major benefits for producers and consumers in business and industry, with competition driving prices down, and at the same time rewarding firms that improve efficiency and quality. The defining illusion of the last twenty years is the belief that similar gains can be achieved through markets in the public sector. Margaret Thatcher's Conservative governments, increasingly influenced by the neo-liberal[3] idea that the state should be active in creating individuals who are enterprising and competitive entrepreneurs, began by privatising public utilities but swiftly moved on to apply market disciplines to areas like health and education (Olssen, 1996). The English market in education was established in the years following the 1988 Reform Act, through a combination of open enrolment, Local Management of Schools (LMS), and nationally published performance tables.

In this new, commercialised world, parents are expected to respond like supermarket shoppers, choosing between effective and less effective institutions so that the best schools succeed while the rest hasten to improve or close for want of customers. The market is supposed to subject schools and teachers to competition, so that they improve their effectiveness continually and close the performance gap between rich and poor. Policy-makers believe so strongly in the virtues of markets, competitive individualism and enterprise that they do not doubt that monetary gain and self advancement are better motivators than the ethic of public service, and seem unconcerned that schools now serve individuals rather than neighbourhoods, and have struggled to preserve the values of community and fraternity.

The survival of the market-fixation after the 2008 crash is a measure of the neo-liberal illusions that dominate elite thinking, and of the depth of the problem for policy-makers who wish to carve space for fresh ideas. David Hare's play *The Power of Yes* at the National Theatre reflects on this triumph of illusion over reality. Before the 15th September 2008, he suggests, the markets and banks were like a ship in apple-pie order. The decks are cleaned, the metal is burnished – the only thing nobody mentions is that the vessel is being driven at full speed towards an iceberg. Politicians believed in a magic porridge pot of credit, and trusted an inner circle of bankers who arranged an endless stream of cash to fund public projects.

The perceived benefits of competition seemed so great that serious people no longer questioned the wisdom of the market. It became an article of faith that when schools compete with one another the lessons must get better. There is no evidence, however, that markets have produced an overall improvement in the quality of teaching. Instead, they have stimulated an unequal competition that has increased rather than reduced the consequences of poverty, and have distracted attention from the complex problems associated with ensuring equitable provision. The creation of academies and faith schools, together with the expansion of the specialist colleges programme, has further exacerbated the problem of unfair competition, with enhanced buildings, facilities and funding associated with some establishments but not others.

3. Central regulation and inspection ensure high standards of quality and performance

Although policy-makers were attracted by the idea of giving school leaders new managerial freedom through LMS, they were equally determined to impose a strong regulatory framework to guide teachers along the path towards efficiency and effectiveness. Unfortunately, the assumption that a centralised National Curriculum, accompanied by a rigorous assessment system, must improve the quality of education and raise standards of school and student performance, is another illusion. There is no reason why changes in subject content and in assessment techniques should enable teachers and children to do better, and after a long experiment there is no evidence that they have done so. We have standardised school knowledge to match the prejudices of the most conservative elements in politics and the media, and in the process have taught our teachers to do as they are told rather than think for themselves. It is ironic that successful schools are now offered the opportunity to raise standards by departing from the National Curriculum regulations, especially as readers of the latest version are invited to 'see the curriculum as something to embrace, support and celebrate' (Qualifications and Curriculum Authority (QCA), 2007a:2).

Ofsted, created by Kenneth Clarke as Secretary of State in 1992, is the most powerful of the regulatory bodies that has emerged since 1988. Successive ministers and most Members of Parliament have succumbed to the illusion that challenging inspection visits and strongly worded reports are valuable aids to improvement, especially in areas where social geography has produced conditions that exert immense pressure on students and staff (House of Commons, 1999). Despite massive expenditure on Ofsted and other agencies and initiatives, however, the number of struggling schools is much the same as before. Very few of the 2 per cent of secondary schools subjected to the bracing experience of special measures have contrived a long-term improvement in their GCSE results (Fitz *et al*, 2000). The gap between less successful schools and the rest is even wider than it was twenty years ago, reflecting a broader trend towards social inequality.

The government's reliance on national agencies and officials has also contributed to the emergence of a growing democratic deficit. Parents, children and even education authorities find themselves ignored or discounted as central authorities intervene to micro-manage institutions in Ofsted categories (e.g special measures) or to impose new types of school (e.g academies). We have a system that is more compliant than before but also less accountable to local elected members and their communities.

4. Successful leaders transform their schools and change the system

Since Tony Blair's election in 1997, leadership has become an increasingly important policy theme, with heads expected to transform their schools and ensure big improvements in examination results. Policymakers and academics pronounce with confidence and authority on the characteristics and styles believed to make schools more effective and students more assiduous. Outstanding heads are said to motivate and encourage their colleagues, lead by example, extend leadership opportunities, promote professional development, encourage initiative, praise generously, know the names of learners, involve the community, and build and empower teams (Matthews, 2009). The NCSL claim that 'high performing and rapidly improving schools are characterised by learning-centred leaders' and that these leaders concentrate on 'influencing what happens inside classrooms' to improve the quality of teaching and pupils' learning (2007:8).

School effectiveness research, case studies and inspection evidence are regularly cited in support of these assertions. The NCSL, for example, endorses the results of Viviane Robinson's meta-analysis of 26 schools, 18 of them conducted in the United States (US) (Matthews, 2009). Robinson (2007) identifies five dimensions that improve student outcomes, especially leaders who participate with teachers in professional learning (large effect), and also plan, coordinate and evaluate teaching and the curriculum (moderately large effect).

The government is insistent about the transformative power of leadership, and emphasises the role of heads and teachers in driving their schools and children towards ever more impressive levels of performance, but as we shall see in chapter 5, there is almost no evidence that this can be done. Dramatic gains are expected but even leadership optimists acknowledge that the effects on student learning are small and indirect. At best, leadership explains no more than between 3 to 5 per cent of the variation in student learning (Leithwood and Riehl, 2003).

The leadership illusion is attractive because it seems to confirm the common sense belief that heads and principals make a crucial difference to the quality of school life. Whether this is true or not, no link

9

has been established between leadership behaviour and student performance, as measured by tests and examinations.

5. Best practice in teaching and organisation can be transferred from one site to another so that every school performs at a high level

Policy makers and school improvement enthusiasts share the potent illusion that 'best practice' recommendations can be applied in every classroom, so that standards rise and no child is left behind. Studies from around the world have shown that schools with better than expected examination results share similar organisational characteristics. The conclusion has been drawn that these characteristics (e.g organic management, clear vision, academic focus) explain how high performing schools achieve better results; and that less effective schools can improve by adapting their internal processes to match those at more successful rivals. School leaders should aim to raise standards and improve performance by applying research-based recommendations. Effectiveness experts are confident that local conditions are unimportant.

There is little evidence, however, that one set of teaching methods (e.g taking account of learning styles) produces consistently better results than others or that lesson formats can be transferred successfully from one school to another, regardless of context. Recommendations based on research into classroom effectiveness seem essentially tautological – if you want your school to be more effective you should copy the characteristics of schools that are more effective. There are very few examples of schools that have succeeded in moving from one level of effectiveness to another (Barker, 2008).

Grade Inflation

The belief that a combination of leadership and best practice teaching can enable schools to overcome disadvantage and transform students' opportunities and outcomes has been sustained by grade inflation, the educational equivalent of the rising stock and housing markets that preceded the 2008 crash. Given the extent of the grade inflation that has marked New Labour's period in office, schools were bound to improve in terms of test and examination results. These results have been treated as independent and objective measures of success when they are in reality an integral feature of the government's programme.

10

Just as rising house prices created the illusion of value on which further borrowing and spending were based, the increase in the numbers participating in examinations and securing better grades has encouraged policy-makers to believe in their own reforms. Since the 1960s, the remarkable expansion of the sixteen plus, sixth form and university degree examination cohorts has produced results very different from the predicted 'more means worse'. As more and more students from the lower deciles of the normal distribution curve have participated in academic courses and examinations, the results have got better and better. In 1990, 34 per cent of students achieved 5 GCSE A*- C grades. In 2008, 65 per cent reached the same benchmark. In 1991, 78 per cent of Advanced (A) Level candidates passed the examination, and 12 per cent obtained A grades. In 2008, 97 per cent passed, with 25 per cent awarded grade A. Although student numbers in British universities have risen from 185,000 (1966) to almost 2 million (2008), the percentage achieving good results has improved, with 62 per cent now obtaining first and upper second-class degrees (BBC News, 2008, 2009; DCSF, 2008).

Critics complain that these apparently excellent results are tainted by the suspicion of manipulation behind the scenes – has the assessment coinage been debased? The annual debate about standards illustrates the difficulty of knowing whether improved grades are due to better learning and teaching or arise from variations in the test and examination regime. The official performance tables are produced by an assessment apparatus entirely controlled by the government, however, and a tell-tale indicator of their unreliability is that since the late 1960s the number of students qualified for admission increased at approximately the rate university places were provided. In other words, performance data cannot be used reliably to judge the success of the system of which they are an intrinsic component. There is a widespread reluctance to believe in results that seem too good to be true.

Contradictions of Reform

The five illusions have exerted, nevertheless, a formative influence on education policy for over twenty years. An intellectual and emotional climate has been created within which successive governments have increased their power, enabling Secretaries of State and their agents to intervene in the smallest details of children's lives. Tony Blair, as opposition leader and as Prime Minister, insisted that education was his only real priority. His attitude reflected and encouraged policy-makers' preoccupation with school reform – always to increase central control and to pressurise teachers and children, whose moral and intellectual deficits were perceived to be responsible for the nation's economic weaknesses.

As a senior government adviser, first in the Department for Education and Employment (DfEE), and later as Head of the Prime Minister's Delivery Unit, Michael Barber emerged as a Robespierre-like figure[4], on a mission to produce a utopian, failure-free world through a 'shock therapy' combination of targets, league tables and inspection (Barber, 2008). Barber's emphasis on results as being the only acceptable evidence of progress towards so-called challenging targets, produced a performance apparatus with a life and logic of its own. Education was reduced to material that could be churned out, tested, graded and counted because it became more important to measure and compare results than to capture qualitative aspects of students' learning. Schools were conditioned to be more concerned with their accountability, especially to visiting Ofsted inspectors, than with traditional conceptions of liberal education.

Successive education acts have transferred responsibility for the direction and control of learning and assessment from schools and teachers to national agencies, creating in the process an immensely expensive and unproductive bureaucracy and reducing the professional ground available for even the best teachers. The tests once set and marked by subject teachers and communicated to parents in end of term reports, for example, have become a multi-million pound industry, directed and regulated by government ministers and their officials, and the source of profit for numerous private contractors.

The policy architecture that has emerged since 1988 seems rational and coherent, with the constituent parts contributing to a wise plan for school improvement. Like businesses, schools compete in an education marketplace subject to regulation by government agencies. Targets are set and managers are held accountable. The trouble is that this apparently logical model has evolved over time and has absorbed within

12

itself the miscellaneous, often contradictory impulses and ideologies that shaped particular initiatives and goals (Ball, 1999). Policy has been mediated through 'deeply embedded norms and assumptions' so that governments have been unable 'to exert much control over the combination of practices which are likely to result' (Newman, 2001:27).

The government agencies responsible for managing the system have been reinvented on numerous occasions, and their duties and objectives have been varied to suit new circumstances. The National Curriculum that emerged in the late 1980s has been regularly amended, slimmed and rewritten to accommodate a variety of pressures and policy fashions. The latest version invites schools 'to build their own curriculum that reflects their local context and meets their learners' needs, capabilities and aspirations' (QCA, 2007a:3) but the accompanying programmes of study and attainment targets prescribe expected skills and knowledge in great detail (QCA, 2007b).

The result is that the system has been undermined from within by its own increasing contradictions. The 1988 Education Reform Act emphasised self-managing schools and the importance of heads becoming entrepreneurs, set free from local authority (LA) control and released from the dead hand of state bureaucracy. The same legislation also concentrated immense power in the hands of the Secretary of State, and imposed curriculum and assessment regulations on the very schools that were supposed to be self-managing and free. Schools were allowed to compete in everything except education.

The Conservative reforms, followed by New Labour's determination to identify and transform poor performance, have created a coercive, top-down, compliance-driven system. The accountability arrangements established through Ofsted after 1992 placed heads in an anxiety-inducing free market environment where they could be named and shamed, although they had no control over the nature of the education for which they were responsible and enjoyed so-called 'freedom' only in matters that were of marginal significance.

The motivational psychology implicit in the Ofsted approach is at variance with other New Labour schemes. The NCSL has implemented training programmes that encourage authoritative rather than coercive leadership styles and celebrate the value of flexibility, responsibility and risk-taking. The NCSL now promotes transformational and distributed leadership as essential for school success (NCSL, 2001). The political leadership of the education service has seldom acted on these principles, however, and the current faith in visionary, transformational leaders is inconsistent with the standardised national requirements vigorously policed by Ofsted.

Policies that promote centralised, national solutions are also inconsistent with the complexity of school provision that has emerged. Since 2005, the aim has been to create choice and diversity through a mix of faith and specialist schools, privately sponsored city academies and a remainder of struggling post-comprehensives. Competition has been increased but since 2002 schools have also been urged to collaborate in federations to raise standards, promote inclusion, and find new ways of approaching teaching and learning.

Critics argue that while New Labour has strengthened the central apparatus of inspection and control, it has also intensified the complexity of policy-making and has encouraged the operational fragmentation of public services (Deem *et al*, 2007). These tensions and contradictions suggest that government policies and practices are not as aligned and mutually complementary as they appear. The gleaming science of large-scale school reform has become more inconsistent and incoherent with time and has contributed to the widespread perception that the current policy regime has come to the end of its useful life (Newman, 2001).

Fading Magic

The impression that the performance apparatus has become ineffective as well as unsustainably expensive is confirmed by other developments. Large-scale school reform around the world seems to have stalled, while concerns about the limited gains achieved are so acute, especially on the political right, that there are demands for even more rigorous reforms to transform the classroom and raise standards. Better English test and examination results look less good when they are compared with those of our OECD partners and suggest that the return generated by massively increased spending since 1997 has been much less than expected. Parents and teachers seem no more satisfied than before, despite the remarkable growth of opportunity and apparent choice in

14

sixth forms and in higher education institutions (Smithers, 2007; Hoyle and Wallace, 2007).

Top policy advisers accept that progress has been disappointing and are losing faith in grand, one-size fits all solutions. The centralised assessment regime is near collapse, after a well-targeted campaign by primary heads infuriated by the poor reliability of the tests themselves as well as by a spectacular marking fiasco that led to the resignation of Ken Boston, Chief Executive of the QCA. Ed Balls, as Secretary of State, responded in October 2008 by declaring an end to mandatory national testing at Key Stage 3. Michael Gove, Shadow Secretary of State, proposes to discontinue the Key Stage 2 tests, and to replace them with a diagnostic examination for newly arrived students in secondary schools.

The consequences are potentially profound. What is the future of the performance tables when essential data streams cease? How can progress be measured if there are no reliable benchmarks for earlier stages of children's education? Can education markets survive the loss of reliable comparative data? Like a giant Ponzi[5] investment scam, exposed by the credit crunch, the government programme to raise standards has been undermined by fears that better results may be a product of grade inflation, and that even these possibly fraudulent gains have been achieved by narrowing the curriculum, bullying teachers and inducing unnecessary levels of student stress.

Observers have begun to recognise the way the government's ceaseless initiatives have become counter-productive. Teachers are barely able to remember what they are supposed to do with one cunning scheme, before having to embark on the next. There is too much to do, so that schools and teachers become selective when they interpret and implement policy. Ministers scramble to leave an individual mark, as if lasting and valuable changes can be brought about in every school in the country without concentrated and sustained attention to every level of implementation. Thoughtful advisers have learned lessons in change management from their experience with top down reform, but many agencies and officials continue to behave as if Seymour Sarason (1996) had not provided an exceptionally good account of why US Federal government education programmes failed in the 1970s. John Dunford

(2009b:14) argues that Ministers should resist the temptation to introduce more eye-catching initiatives and let educational institutions focus instead 'on the core mission of learning and teaching'. The national government educational apparatus is an important obstacle to further progress.

Conservative policy rhetoric and proposals have begun to exploit this trend in public and professional opinion. Michael Gove (2009) is anxious to emphasise his party's commitment to 'greater freedom for professionals' and his belief in the advantages of freedom from central control, although long-serving teachers may recall an earlier period when the Conservatives imposed the bureaucratic system that has become the problem they now condemn. Gove declares his support for the cause of 'greater autonomy, in the context of deeper collaboration' and claims that school freedoms are 'central to Conservative education plans' (2009:28). The pendulum is swinging, even if its ultimate direction remains unclear.

School Reform – Flawed Assumptions

These causes of dissatisfaction with school reform, the long term implications of the financial and economic crisis, and the prospect of a British General Election, have created a rare opportunity to reinvent education policy by learning from past mistakes, and to reconsider how to encourage teachers and students to do their best. Within the next year or so, policy-makers must ask themselves fundamental questions about the nature and form of future education provision and find answers that are both more ambitious and more realistic than New Labour's expensive, top-down, target-obsessed regime. The urgent priority is to transform school reform and to create the conditions in which learning and teaching can flourish, and where young people's moral and intellectual growth is not overwhelmed by narrow economic considerations and the skills agenda. The main obstacle is the tenacity of long-held illusions.

As we have seen, five fundamentally flawed, essentially illusory propositions have driven school reform since at least 1988. Despite their transparent failure, they have continued to exert a stranglehold on the education policy agenda. Serious politicians are afraid to challenge the main tenets of school reform and dare not relax their unrelenting pursuit of outstanding results and ratings for all. They know that the popular press is poised to exploit bad news about standards, so continue to promote a simple story of tough love, rigorous systems and ever-improving results. Even the schools are locked into the improvement illusion the performance regime has induced, however painful and unrealistic it may seem to many teachers. Perceptive observers are also reluctant to admit that the Emperor is completely naked, because everyone else seems to believe that his clothes have been spun from the finest thread imaginable.

These propositions also permeate the DNA of agencies like Ofsted, the QCA, the NCSL and the TDA. After years of top-down, target-led reform, the government policy apparatus has become impervious to alternative strategies, and is unable to question its own fundamental assumptions, not least because so much has been invested in them. This frozen mindset has become a serious liability.

This book aims, therefore, to challenge the illusions and the flawed assumptions on which they are based, in order to stimulate a wide-ranging policy debate. As the pendulum swings, future ministers and their advisers need an improved understanding of what has gone wrong, as well as access to constructive suggestions about how to improve the quality of education for all our children. Chapters 2-6 investigate the weaknesses and limitations of the five school reform propositions and examine their impact on schools and classrooms. Chapters 7 and 8 seek alternative, improved foundations for a transformed approach to education policy.

Chapter 2 (Must the Disadvantaged Fail?) presents evidence that school reform has failed to improve the relative success and life chances of disadvantaged students and communities. Why and how does poverty hinder progress so much? Is there a solution?

Chapter 3 (Markets and Competition) examines the argument that the market disciplines introduced by the 1988 Education Act have improved education by increasing choice, freedom, competition and equity.

Chapter 4 (Imagine an End to Failure) explores how central government agencies impact on local education, through a case study of St Michael's Church School in the East Midlands. This struggling Church of England comprehensive, named and shamed by Ofsted, was swiftly afterwards fast-tracked for Academy status, against the wishes of a majority of parents and children. The chapter analyses the limitations of our top-down apparatus of school reform. Why does there seem no end to failure?

Chapter 5 (Bastards and Prophets) examines the extent to which visionary leaders can be expected to build system-wide success, despite the organisational complexity and fragmentation induced by New Public Management (NPM). Case studies of six outstanding school leaders are presented. Are they 'bastard leaders' trapped in an eventually futile quest for better examination results, or can they become prophets of transformation?

Chapter 6 (Best Practice) considers the claim that 'we know what works' and that 'best practice' recommendations can be transferred from one setting to another, regardless of context, with a potentially transformational impact on effectiveness and performance. The classroom level influence of the performance regime is considered – what are the gains and losses of hyper-accountability?

Chapter 7 (Progressive Alternatives) returns to the formative days of comprehensive education. Although progressive ideas were discredited in the culture wars of the 1970s, the child-centred, democratic critique of traditional schooling has contemporary value and relevance. The philosopher John Macmurray's rejection of the self, as an isolated individual who should pursue instrumental goals, is assessed as a possible foundation for a new policy approach, with a strong emphasis on the personal and social growth of individuals, families and their communities.

Chapter 8 (Transforming School Reform) explores the fears and hopes that may influence the future and draws upon progressive insights to identify four strategic priorities for change.

2

Must the Disadvantaged Fail?

Progress and Poverty

The government's consistent denial that social environments have an important impact on performance has stifled debate about learning and relative poverty, and has frustrated educators anxious to reduce inequality and to improve the quality of education for ordinary children. This chapter explores the reasons why deprived children fail to progress as school reformers expect, and why disadvantage has frustrated all the schemes and initiatives that have been deployed against it. Social variables are too significant to be ignored and there can be no hope of improving education until we have understood and found ways to deal with the pernicious problems of poverty and social disadvantage.

Chris Moore, principal of Hillside, a struggling city school in the Midlands, had no doubt that urban deprivation was a major influence on the quality of learning. He found that the 'wild' behaviour of a small minority of children in his school was having a disproportionately negative effect, with lessons disrupted and teachers distracted from their classroom duties. Moore worried about the 'sheer number of serious student and family problems' and feared that he would be overwhelmed by a caseload of disturbed and violent children. It seemed that his job was less to do with improving Hillside than with keeping the lid on families who 'overspill their neighbours, school and community' (Chris Moore Diary, quoted in Barker, 2003).

Moore's experience would be recognised and understood by many heads and teachers who work with disadvantaged children. Their experience has taught them about the challenges of helping young people whose growth has been impaired by various types of deprivation. They are not surprised that many poor children are intellectually and emotionally less than well equipped for school and often struggle to keep pace with their peers from more privileged backgrounds. They are not surprised that education markets work against schools in deprived areas and have widened the gap between rich and poor. Their practical wisdom tells them that the five reform propositions discussed in chapter 1 are absurd illusions, based on the wilful denial of the complexity of social reality.

Policy-makers have been reluctant to accept these pessimistic conclusions about the impact of disadvantage, however, and have aligned themselves with a long line of reformers who have believed that education can change individual lives and compensate for negative social influences. Henry George, the famous American campaigner for social justice, dedicated his book *Progress and Poverty* (2005) 'to those who, seeing the vice and misery that spring from the unequal distribution of wealth and privilege, feel the possibility of a higher social state and would strive for its attainment.' This idealistic response to inequality and poverty was similar to that of many crusaders for working class education in the period after the 1870 Education Act, who were convinced that appropriate instruction for the masses would create a better society. Reformers, like Robert Owen (1969:99), were persuaded that:

> Any general character, from the best to the worst, from the most ignorant to the most enlightened, may be given to any community, even to the world at large, by the application of proper means.

As a result, schools have been expected to improve and even transform society, in addition to introducing their pupils to the knowledge and skills necessary for future employment. Contemporary models of school effectiveness and transformation belong, therefore, to a long tradition of great expectations. Visions of a better, more educated society, within our reach if not our grasp, haunt the landscape of school reform.

Poverty has proved resilient, however, resisting periods of prosperity as well as the varied exertions of the welfare state. Council estates in employment free zones have replaced the deadly industrial slums of the early nineteenth century, while textile sweatshops have found new sources of cheap labour, at home and abroad. The thresholds and meanings of poverty have changed, so that social analysts have adopted cautious terms like 'relative poverty', 'disadvantage' and 'social exclusion' to define the object of their concern. But the irreducible phenomenon of poverty persists in the lives of millions of people, who are restricted in ways that are sometimes obvious and sometimes obscure.

The unresolved policy puzzle is that education has made so little impression on the 'unequal distribution of wealth and privilege'; has not brought about a 'higher social state'; and has failed to give a particularly 'enlightened' character to many communities. Unfettered access to high quality education and training in the modern period is supposed to have improved everyone's skills, knowledge and aspirations, including those from lower income groups. Instead, the many avatars of poverty and disadvantage seem to have been ingenious in finding ways to undermine the possibility of progress. Bernstein's (1970:344) observation that 'education cannot compensate for society' suggests that the formative relationship between school and community is the reverse of that anticipated by campaigners for educational and social reform.

Our ability to research, understand and mediate the ways in which poverty hinders progress has been constrained by an impasse between two fundamental positions. For two decades, policy-makers have rejected or ignored strong evidence that disadvantage is a negative factor shaping learning and results, claiming instead that LAs and teachers use poverty as an excuse for poor academic results. School performance has been measured and judged with scant concern for social context or student intake, although New Labour does support disadvantaged families through tax credits, and with initiatives like Sure Start that acknowledge and seek to remedy the effects and impact of social exclusion. So-called 'value added' measures compare students with similar prior attainment but do not take account of disadvantage. Sociologists and historians of education have been equally firm and repetitive in countering that schools cannot overcome or 'compensate' for the consequences of inequality and poverty. Like many others, Lowe (1997) argues that the education system is more effective at perpetuating disadvantage than remedying defects in the social structure.

Access and Opportunity: A Study in Failure?

Reformers, from Robert Owen to the present day, have seen poverty as a serious obstacle to national efficiency, and their policy recommendations have been influenced by human capital theory as much as by moral objections to squalor and wasted lives. As globalisation has gathered momentum and international economic competitiveness has grown, governments have turned to education as the means for increasing the number of skilled employees available to service the needs of industry and commerce. The Conservatives argued in 1994 (*Our Children's Future*, quoted in Bell and Stevenson, 2006:47) that: 'Our future prosperity as a nation depends on how well our schools, in partnership with parents, prepare young people for work'. By 1998 Labour was equally convinced that:

> Investment in human capital will be the foundation of success in the knowledge-based global economy. We need a well-educated, well-equipped labour force. (DfEE, 1998)

As a result of this imperative, reforming administrations have seen the solution to poverty in terms of better access and opportunity for ordinary people, whose learning and self-improvement should lead to increased individual and national efficiency. Comprehensive schools were introduced in an egalitarian attempt to remove barriers to full participation in secondary education. Following the Education Reform Act in 1988, positivist, scientific, mass-produced solutions have been adopted to deal with the complex institutional and classroom level obstacles to effective learning and improved student performance. Since 1997, New Labour has pursued both strands, by using pressure and support to ensure that schools become more effective and productive, and by adopting social inclusion policies intended to enable the disadvantaged to access the many new educational opportunities that have been made available.

The 2004 Children's Act established an elaborate apparatus to ensure that children were helped to be *healthy*, to be *safe*, to *enjoy and achieve*, to *make a positive contribution*, and to *achieve economic well-being*. Agencies and services were reorganised and national priority targets were announced to deal with issues like obesity, bullying, drugs and literacy. The *Every Child Matters* agenda includes, under the 'enjoy and achieve' heading, the expectation that all children should 'Achieve stretching national educational targets' at primary and secondary school (Department for Education and Skills (DfES), 2004:9).

Governments have persisted with the twin track policies of improving access and increasing effectiveness (and have remained in denial about the continuing influence of social variables) for two main reasons. Policy-makers do not understand why the combination of equal opportunity and classroom science has failed; and they are unimpressed by their critics' insistence on the inevitability of social and cultural reproduction. Twelve years of the 'Education, Education, Education' mantra should have reduced the performance gap between advantaged and disadvantaged young people, opening the route to participation and success for all. Once all children have fair access to good quality schools, effective teaching and many opportunities for success, why should there be a problem?

The trouble is that the social variables involved operate in ways that are chaotic and complex, so it is very difficult to produce a convincing, coherent explanation of how disadvantaged families and their children are less able to benefit from educational opportunities, even when the teaching is very good indeed. The least well off seem almost to spurn success, an attitude beyond the comprehension of those in higher social groups. Ministers persevere with the 'lessons' of effectiveness research for want of something better and continue to believe that further instalments of reform can achieve the ultimate breakthrough to a better society. Despite the failure of the banks, economic policy continues in the free market mould for much the same reason.

There is abundant evidence, however, that this persistence is misguided. Relative disadvantage has increased rather than reduced. BBC News (2004) lists the following indicators, suggesting that despite decades of sustained economic growth, social progress has been less than generally believed:

- One fifth of the UK's poorest households do not have any type of bank or building society account. (Source: Joseph Rowntree Foundation – Monitoring Poverty and Social Exclusion 2002)

- A childless couple with over £805 in net income (weekly) – or a combined salary of £57,000 – are in the top 5 per cent of earners in the UK. (Source: Department for Work and Pensions 2001-2)

- The top tenth of the UK population now receives a greater share of total net income than the entire bottom half. (Source: Department for Work and Pensions 2001-2)

- In 2001-2, over 40 per cent of people in lone-parent households were in the poorest fifth of the UK population and 73 per cent in the poorest two-fifths. (Source: Department for Work and Pensions 2001-2)

- In 2001-2, ethnic minority households made up 8.6 per cent of the UK population but also made up 15 per cent of the poorest fifth. (Source: Department for Work and Pensions 2001-2)

These examples illustrate a marked United Kingdom trend towards increasing inequality. The Institute for Fiscal Studies measures the spread of incomes over time using the so-called 'Gini coefficient', with the value for each year expressed as a proportion of that for 1974, the base year (Clark, 2009). Table 1 below shows the index figure for selected years between 1974 and 2006. Clark (2009:20) claims that the increase in the UK income gap 'has been the sharpest in the developed world' and is most probably the result of government policy changes, since there are many countries where differentials are more or less unchanged. In the UK, the richest fifth of the population has 7.2 times more income than the poorest fifth, a ratio that is one of the highest in the free world.

Income differentials are greater, relative poverty has grown, and the sides of the social pyramid are steeper. There is also very little evidence that education policy has been successful in overcoming the effects of increasing relative disadvantage or stimulating social mobility. In 2007, 68 per cent of students from better off families achieved 5 GCSE A*-C grades, compared with 57 per cent the previous year, while only 25 per cent of the least well-off students reached the good GCSE benchmark, down from 29 per cent in 2006. At the age of 7, 93 per cent of the most

Year	1974	1978	1980	1989	1996	2000	2006
Index	100	95	103	130	133	141	140

Table 1: Institute for Fiscal Studies, Measure of Income Spread

affluent students reach the expected standard for reading, while only 73 per cent of the least affluent attain this level. When children are divided into 10 bands of affluence and deprivation, achievement rises with wealth in every subject and at every level. At primary school, those living in the most deprived areas form the largest social group. The number in this deprived group continuing to study beyond age 16 declines by about 90 per cent, and they have the lowest average A-level points score (BBC News, 2007).

The following example (see chart 1, overleaf) shows how disadvantage impacts on individual schools, frustrating efforts to improve their effectiveness and producing a local education market that magnifies the consequences of inequality. Chart 1 shows the percentage achieving 5 GCSE grades A*-C (white squares) and those entitled to Free School Meal (FSM) (black triangles) at 17 schools in an urban district in the north of England.

The schools (horizontal axis) are positioned 1 (top) – 17 (bottom) by their mean percentage achieving 5 GCSE higher grades for the six years 1994-1999. School 1 averaged 61 per cent higher grades and 6 per cent free meals; School 17 averaged 19 per cent higher grades and 38 per cent free meals. Patterns of achievement were remarkably stable throughout the period. In GCSE terms, schools 1-5 were consistently more effective than schools 6-17. The top five outperformed all the others by a wide margin through the six years. Schools 8-14, operating with similar FSM entitlements, jockeyed for individual position within a narrow band (15% to 34% 5 A*-C grades). Schools 15, 16 and 17 were always at the bottom of the local table. None of the schools achieved a breakthrough to a higher level of effectiveness during the period 1994 – 1999, despite considerable pressure from government agencies to do so.

Chart 1 suggests that the key difference between the supposedly effective and less effective schools is social background, as measured by eligibility for free meals. Although FSM is an unsatisfactory poverty measure, liable to over and under-state disadvantage in a particular district, the level of entitlement at an individual school provides a consistent indicator of the social effects believed to explain a high percentage of the performance differences between schools (Scheerens,

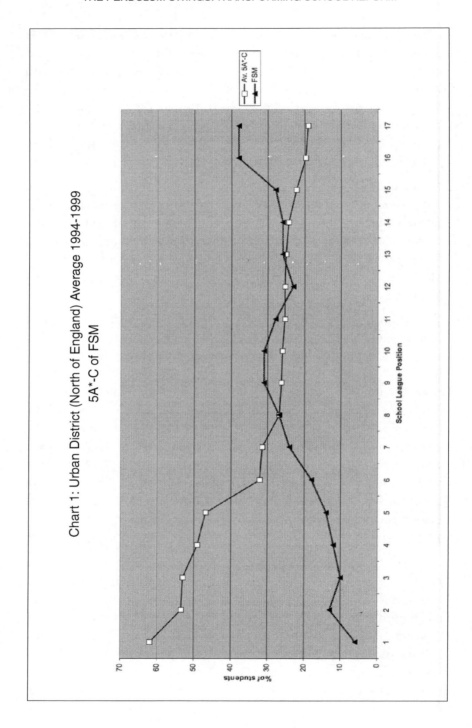

Chart 1: Urban District (North of England) Average 1994-1999
5A*-C of FSM

1989; Creemers, 1994). FSM uptake at the effective schools (1-5) is relatively low. At the ineffective schools (15, 16, 17) the figure is much higher. Once the annual increase in national performance is excluded from the calculation, improved results seem remarkably hard to achieve, whatever the competitive pressure. Schools with a similar FSM entitlement achieve consistently similar outcomes, with minor annual fluctuations. Variations in school intake are more important, therefore, than institutional factors in explaining differences in results between schools, and contribute to the formation of a hierarchy that reflects the local distribution of inequality and disadvantage.

Assumptions based on effectiveness research have conditioned policy-makers and the public at large to admire schools and students with good results and to attribute success to the quality of the institution concerned. Why can't all schools be as good as this one? The evidence suggests, however, that social factors account for an important slice of the apparently marked variations between schools. Good results are more closely associated with middle class neighbourhoods than with the organisational characteristics of any particular school. This conclusion confirms Jencks *et al* (1972:256), whose substantial data indicated that 'the character of a school's output depends largely on a single input, namely the characteristics of the entering children.'

Deep, historically rooted social and cultural variables influence our chances of success and seem beyond the reach of attempts to fine-tune classrooms and teaching methods (Bernstein, 1970; Lowe, 1997). Given these consistent findings, Thrupp (1999) believes it is unrealistic to expect the education system to produce radical change in the relative performance of students from impoverished backgrounds. Even when schools and colleges improve their effectiveness, increased efficiency seems unlikely to produce a disproportionate benefit for those who have already demonstrated a less strong disposition to learn.

Policies that promote school effectiveness and social inclusion seem unlikely, therefore, to reverse current trends. National agencies may be reluctant to recognise the impact of poverty on learning, but increased inequality and disadvantage demonstrate that the government's education and inclusion policies have failed to improve outcomes for the children at greatest risk of social exclusion. 'Stretching national targets' have proved counter-productive, increasing the scope for failure and compounding existing social divisions. There is no realistic prospect of improvement in the education of young people from less prosperous circumstances until policy-makers acknowledge the depth and complexity of underlying social issues. There is an urgent need to research and better understand the relationship between disadvantage and learning, and to use the knowledge gained to inform the reconstruction of social organisations so that they better serve the needs of the people.

The Sociology of Education

Sociologists once provided convincing evidence that pre-existing class differences are highly significant for educational outcomes. David Hargreaves (1982) summarises a range of conclusions established in the 1960s and 1970s. The children of parents in manual occupations are likely to be in lower streams and to perform less well than their non-manual contemporaries. There are marked differences between children from upper and lower social groups, in terms of their own attitudes and aspirations, as well as their outcomes. Manual workers' children tend to be underestimated by their teachers, to leave school early, and to drop out of further and higher education.

Class is a slippery phenomenon, however, and the registrar general's categories can mask complex differentiation within the social landscape. As Hargreaves observes, sociological writing often does less than justice to the changes that have taken place in the class structure since the 1970s. The UK manufacturing base was eroded during the 1980s, with the coal, steel and textile industries much reduced in size and economic importance. The trade unions were weakened as much by the loss of members as by legislation that removed their legal immunities. Social commentators, attracted by the idea of an affluent, classless society, have increasingly emphasised the role of the individual and discounted evidence of inequality. Even so, Hargreaves' carefully drawn contrast between the 'large detached houses in extensive, pleasant grounds' and 'tightly packed treeless streets' suggests that at least some of society's divisions persist (1982:13).

Class-based explanations of pupils' resistant behaviour observed at school continue to make sense. Sennett and Cobb (1972) explain how 'ordinary working class boys' may build a 'counter-culture of dignity'

28

based on male solidarity, and define themselves in opposition to teachers and classroom learning. Gilbert and Gilbert (1998) place a similar emphasis on the extent to which working class males are pre-occupied with their 'masculinity' and avoid behaviour that might lead them to be perceived as 'feminine' by other boys. Peer pressure discourages conscientious engagement with school, while even committed students from low status backgrounds may pay a significant price for their success (Hoskins, 2010). Willis (1977) argues that lower class boys become 'oppositional', not so much because they come from disadvantaged backgrounds but because their class values provide a resource in constructing a counter-culture that salvages dignity from their treatment by teachers. As Kirk argues:

> The ramifications of class inequality and difference cut into subjective experiences and bury themselves deep, and this in turn has profound implications for how people see themselves, others and the world. (2007:5)

Official concern about the impact of social and cultural influences on learning has been limited to the perceived poor test and examination performance of some ethnic minority students. The Swann Report (1985) considered differences in attainment between ethnic groups and drew particular attention to low qualification levels amongst those from Bangladeshi backgrounds. Haque and Bell (2001) discovered that when adjustments are made for the students' recency of arrival in the UK, their fathers' occupation and their mothers' education, the apparent effects of ethnicity on performance are much less. There is increasing evidence that the performance gaps attributed to ethnicity and gender are much smaller than the marked social class gap at Key Stage 4. White British students living in disadvantaged circumstances are the lowest attaining ethnic group, while Black Caribbean boys remain a cause for concern (Strand, 2008).

Child-raising patterns have been found to vary by social class and ethnicity and this may contribute to variations in young people's response to school. Middle class parents are reported to be heavily involved with their children, adopting a pattern of 'concerted cultivation', while working class families are inclined to leave children to their own devices. Middle class parents talk things through with their children, reasoning with them and expecting them to talk back and question adults in authority. The less well off believe it is up to the teachers to educate their sons and daughters, and are intimidated by authority (Lareau, 2003, quoted in Gladwell, 2008:104).

This is consistent with research into language acquisition and use that emphasises the importance of talk with adults. Significant differences in vocabulary and communication have been identified between middle and working class children. Basil Bernstein (1971) argues that the middle class use an elaborated code, well adapted to academic purposes, while the working class construct meaning with a restricted code that leaves them at a disadvantage in formal settings. More recently, children from deprived backgrounds have been found to arrive at school with a vocabulary of around 500 words, compared with the staggering 6,000 words used by those from more affluent backgrounds (The Reader Online, 2009).

This helps explain how middle class students acquire the attitudes and skills needed to negotiate the system and make it work for them. It also explains why less prepared, less fortunate youngsters are often scared of school. Students told Holt (1964) they were afraid of failing, afraid of being kept back, afraid of being called stupid, afraid of feeling themselves stupid. He was startled by how much fear there is in the classroom and how destructive such feelings are for young people's development. Care and cultivation create incalculable advantages for those who experience them, by providing emotional security through positive interaction with adults, and by encouraging and fostering interests, abilities and practical intelligence.

Class, Health and Violence

Lower social status is also closely associated with a greater incidence of ill health and premature mortality. Chart 2 opposite shows the age standardised mortality rate for men aged 25-64, by Socio-Economic Classification (SEC) 2001-2003 (National Statistics Online, 2009).

All cause mortality for women shows a similar gradient. Although mortality rates have fallen for everyone since 1930, they are now almost three times lower for professional groups than for the unskilled. The gap between the fifth of LAs with the lowest life expectancy and the national average has increased by almost two per cent for males, and by

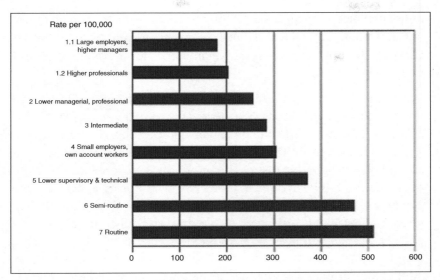

Chart 2: Age-Standardised Mortality Rate by NS-SEC: Men Aged 25-64, England and Wales 2001-03

five per cent for females, between 1997-99 and 2001-03. The infant mortality rate among the 'routine and manual' occupational group was 13 per cent higher than for the total population in 1997-99, and increased to 19 per cent by 2001-03. There are clear links, therefore, between deprivation and factors like physical weakness, stress, reduced immunity, risky health behaviours and illness (Earthy, 2009).

The numbers claiming Incapacity Benefit (2,382,000) and Disability Living Allowance (2,973,540) in 2008 provide a further indication of the impact of ill health on people's lives (Office of National Statistics (ONS), 2009). Poverty may also be embodied in the relative height, weight and health of individual children in lower social groups. Relatively poor physical and mental health contributes in various ways to the disadvantage experienced by many children and reduces their ability to participate effectively in education. Health may affect, for example, attendance, stamina, concentration and perceptions of self-efficacy (Lasker and Mascie-Taylor, 1989). Well-being is an essential precondition for successful education, but is seriously compromised when housing is crowded and unhygienic, where working conditions are potentially dangerous, and where low income and tradition lead to an unhealthy dietary regime. Wilkinson and Pickett (2009) include morbidity and health in their claim that excessively unequal societies (eg. US, UK) produce unexpectedly negative outcomes for everyone, regardless of their social status.

Social and economic disadvantage may also contribute to family disturbance. Elie Godsi (2004) explains dysfunctional behaviour in terms of the close and inextricable links between personal distress and violence, and believes both are an expression of powerlessness and lack of control. People become distressed and harm themselves or others because of what has been done to them. Godsi interprets such behaviour, however self-destructive and self-defeating, as an adaptation to childhood maltreatment, a strategy for coping with misfortune, pain and tragedy. Sexual, physical and emotional abuse produce devastating long-term consequences, while the failure to care for a child's physical, intellectual and emotional needs can inflict permanent damage. Separation and divorce create conditions of uncertainty that may have profound adverse effects. The love and care needed for healthy development tax the time and resources of many families.

Godsi (2004:78-80) describes the increasing number of children looked after by different people and growing up in conditions of instability, neglect and violence. These 'children of chaos' experience a constantly changing family structure, transient or absent fathers, maternal neglect and periods 'in care' or with foster parents. As their maltreatment seldom relates to their actual behaviour, there is a lack of predictability in their lives that harms their ability to form trusting relationships. This may limit their capacity to engage and cooperate with others at school.

Although there is no satisfactory estimate of the number of children whose lives are touched to some degree by maltreatment or neglect, many families struggle with emotional difficulties and disruptive events, including bereavement, separation and divorce. When parents are preoccupied with their own failing relationships, there is a risk that children will lack the nurture needed for the growth of their latent abilities. Distress, neglect and violence are not confined to low status families or particular social conditions, but are more likely to occur in stressful, unsettled circumstances, aggravated by economic deprivation and unemployment. Whatever the cause, the emotional consequences may be permanently damaging for personal development and efficacy.

Social Niches

Class continues, therefore, to provide a valuable framework for understanding social patterns and their impact on learning and on educational institutions. We also need, however, to understand the long, slow, subterranean processes of social evolution and change that produce complexity and difference. What qualities and circumstances enable some individuals and groups to transcend expectations based on class while others fail? The individualist, self-help conception of society as a ladder, with steps rising from the schoolyard to the highest positions in the land, is misleading because it discounts social context and presents instead the image of a one generation miracle, available to all those with serious determination and a modicum of talent and luck.

Malcolm Gladwell's *Outliers* (2008) challenges the conventional belief that successful people leap from rags to riches as a result of their unusual intelligence and ambition. He describes the many economic, social, cultural and circumstantial advantages that accumulate for particular individuals, creating the conditions for their success. Outstanding Canadian hockey players have birthdays earlier in the year, so they are larger and stronger than their peers when junior teams are selected; Bill Gates had access to state-of-the-art computers at the University of Washington and was given almost unlimited programming opportunities; fourteen of the 75 richest people in history are Americans, born within nine years of one another (1831-1840). They were exceptionally well placed to exploit the transformation of the US economy in the 1860s and 1870s. Gladwell himself is an Outlier, helped forward by the 'extraordinary advantage that their little bit of whiteness' gave his African ancestors in Jamaica (2008:280).

Outliers suggests, therefore, the complex interactions of time, place and culture that shape opportunity and success, and shows how personal history enables some individuals to exploit favourable trends and conditions in the environment. A reverse process is easily imagined, with an accumulation of small disadvantages (e.g a dark skin, ill-health) transmitting shadows through successive generations. Daniel Smail (2008) believes that deep history can help us understand this as the outcome of a continuous process of interaction and adaptation between human beings and their environment.

He argues against evolutionary psychology and genetic determinism, claiming instead that many skills and behaviours have genetic and environmental components. Human capacities, he believes, should be seen as genetic potentials that must be triggered by environmental influences. Trillions of synapses are created as juveniles adapt to their environment (e.g learn reading, music, driving, cultural practices), but as unused neurons are discarded from age 8, limited early experience and practice may lessen capacities for which there was genetic potential at birth. There is no 'normal', genetically inspired pattern of human culture and behaviour but endless variation and adaptation, from location to location.

Once society is considered in these evolutionary terms, as the outcome of continuous adaptation between different people and their varied environments, the complex biodiversity of a coral reef ecosystem seems to provide a more suggestive metaphor for the slow processes of social change and decay than a schoolyard ladder, with its assumption of ascent and progress. Individuals, families and groups shift and manoeuvre within the diverse habitats provided by the reef, seeking favourable occupational and geographical niches and adapting to local conditions. Climate, geography, resources and economic systems influence the varied niches available within the reef's evolving structure.

Each niche contains a micro ecosystem of its own, so that trades, crafts and professions expand and contract in response to local conditions, and develop an elaborate internal organisation that reflects changes in the distribution of status and power between members. Over time, niche inhabitants generate distinctive cultures, and adopt attitudes and practices appropriate to their circumstances. Some niches are more influential or prosperous than others (e.g finance, politics; health, education) but there are dominant and less powerful individuals and groups within each (executive, consultant; nurse, secretary). Economic systems may produce high or low levels of differentiation between niches. When conditions are calm and changes come slowly, there may be little movement between niches or within the status hierarchies that have emerged. Turbulence and rapid change create uncertainty but also opportunity, as the balance of the established order is threatened.

The metaphor of a coral reef, with diverse niches to which individuals and groups adapt over time, accommodates a variety of perspectives on social differentiation. Narratives describing the fragmentation of class formations, and their replacement by a proliferation of identities associated with affluence and consumerism, suggest a highly variegated niche structure. Accounts that stress inequality, and claim that cultural, social, linguistic and symbolic forms of capital operate in variable ways to reproduce class differences, envisage less diversity and a common, if subjective, experience of deference, shame, dignity and respect (Sayer, 2005; Kirk, 2007).

Madeleine Bunting provides an example of how social processes may be conceptualised in terms of movement between niches. She is concerned about the fate of members of the skilled working class in Britain, reduced as a proportion of the population from 70 per cent in the 1950s to 15 per cent by 2000. She speculates that these people:

> ...migrated into professional/managerial white-collar work, or moved sideways into retail or on to long-term unemployed/incapacity benefit. Communities that had had very similar income and life experiences were fragmented into widely varying outcomes; some have enjoyed unprecedented consumer and housing wealth, others found themselves stuck and left behind. (Bunting, 2009:25)

This story illustrates the recent fluidity of British society and suggests some of the choices and strategies available to people previously categorised as 'skilled working class'. A post-industrial, service-based economy emerged in this period, destroying traditional formations and niches but also generating new ones. Bunting's description is impressionistic, of course, and lacks the detail needed to establish that all the members of the skilled working class in the 1950s really had 'very similar income and life experiences', and to explain why some individuals and groups thrived and others did not. She is unable to identify the small accumulations of advantage and disadvantage that led to improved niches and wealth for some, while others were left behind.

We may suspect that increased participation in post-compulsory education has consolidated the advantages of some individuals or groups migrating from traditional employment, although the increased number acquiring qualifications has had little impact on productivity or skills (Brown, 2001). Collins (1981) believes the inflation of credentials has contributed more to competition between status groups (not individuals) than to efficiency and growth. This seems to be confirmed by low levels of upward mobility between generations in the UK during the last forty years. Former skilled workers, it seems, are more likely to have migrated laterally between contrasting niches than to have used education as a ladder to climb from low to high status positions (Blanden *et al*, 2005).

Learning and Disadvantage

The ecological notion that individuals and groups accumulate small, and not so small, advantages or disadvantages through their long-term interaction with, and adaptation to, varied niche environments, provides a framework for understanding why some students respond less well to teachers and schools than others. In this light, the less successful are constrained by influences that combine to reduce effective participation in formal learning opportunities, and also to limit the niches and niche positions available to them, even when appropriate credentials have been secured. In education, disadvantage arises from the reciprocal actions of macro (social and cultural), meso (family), and micro (personal) phenomena, not from the operation of a unified gravitational force that exerts equal downward pressure on all the relatively poor. Individual students develop their self-awareness, identity and values through their engagement with people and institutions, forming mindsets that are suited to their niche circumstances. Argyris (1993) describes these mindsets as 'theory-in-use' and believes they can limit thinking and lead to unrecognised errors, especially in new or changed conditions.

Gladwell (2008) believes cultural dispositions can also work to increase or reduce the chances of success or failure. *Outliers* argues that there are important variations between national groups in their attitudes towards authority, uncertainty and individual responsibility, and that these are highly significant for the performance of many tasks, including flying aircraft. He claims that Asian students are more successful in maths tests because their culture, based on generations of painstaking wet-rice agriculture, emphasises hard work and persistence. Gladwell reminds us that people's behaviour is conditioned by particular cultural norms and assumptions that should not be ignored. We need to understand where people are from and the deep influences of location in young people's thinking before we can hope to change their minds.

Accumulations of Disadvantage

As self-awareness and self-knowledge grow, social, cultural and family experiences provide the raw material and emotional charge for young people's subjective constructions of themselves and their lives. Relationships with close adults and peers shape children's perceptions and inform their sense of meaning and identity, for better or for worse. As they reach towards secondary school, they are becoming social commentators and critics, not passive consumers of scientific education. Already they have acclimatised to their niches and have internalised the values, attitudes and interests of their families and communities. They have learned and have come to accept the inevitability their limitations, and understand the language of shame, respect and dignity. Much of their genetic potential has been stimulated or has atrophied, while millions of their unused synapses have been discarded. By age 11, many children have experienced sufficient failure to discount their chances of worthwhile academic results. Others, more favourably endowed and capitalised, inhabit comfortable niches where formal learning is valued and may lead to enhanced skills, knowledge and mobility.

As head of Hillside, Chris Moore recorded his work with children from deprived areas served by the school. The stories of two troubled young women illustrate how disadvantages can accumulate, impede children's engagement with school, and produce mindsets of numbing negativity.

Debbie

Debbie told her mother to fuck off because she'd stolen her fags; she came to school and carried on in the same spirit; bursting into the year head's room and threatening her: 'I want you!' – then stalking off after another teacher tried to calm her down. So I picked her up and between the activities of the day tried to negotiate between the teachers (who see Debbie as an awfully demanding and unresponsive madam who ought to walk) and Debbie and her mother.

Debbie talks persuasively with me; too much so, because what emerges later is she is ultra manipulative and inclined to violence and abuse when she doesn't get what she wants. She is tall; attractive, moral in some of her critique of her mother and pretty immoral in her own behaviour. Her upset is that her mother has just married a 21-year-old boyfriend, who tries to treat her like a daughter. The new husband is only the latest of a series of men. Debbie's sexual jealousy and resentment is tangible; 'I don't have a problem with school; I have a problem at home which I bring to school.'

... Debbie admits she beat up her auntie when she didn't take her ice-skating as promised. 'I banged her head on the floor'; 'She did!' emphasised her mother from the other side of the table. It is a crowded, noisy house and there is not enough space for everyone's needs. Debbie wants to leave; to get away from step-dad; her mother complains about Debbie's abuse of her eight year old brother Sean; Debbie complains that new husband calls his wife a slag and a bitch and threatens to recite all her male associations...

Mother appears at lunchtime and is in a dreadfully distressed state because Debbie has abused her and her husband. She has to be helped over an asthma attack before she is fit to see me (she's covered in blotches, at her wits' end) – and then Debbie batters and clatters at the door for attention. I encourage mum to be in charge – 'we won't exclude her, that's what she wants, take her away to the doctor on medical grounds – something must be done to sort out all these moods'. Mother is very clear that hormones are at the bottom of Debbie being 'evil'; Debbie is keen to get through the door to explain to me that the problem is the family, with her mother and new husband giving her no attention and no money. But after her description of her own capacity for violence I'm not so sure.

Danièle

More student cases today and I finish with a home visit to Danièle and her mother. Plenty of other houses in the street boarded up, wired off or abandoned or demolished. Mother knows Danièle needs help; tells me that she used to attack other children out of the blue, even when very young (aged 6).

Danièle's eyes roll; she has an angry core and could be very dangerous. She is mature for year 8 – her mother agrees that she's grown up in next to no time. But the entanglements with other children keep on happening. She is beyond what teachers can do for her already. She doesn't want to be in school; learning is the last thing on her mind. (Chris Moore Diary, cited in Barker, 2003)

Debbie lives in an unhappy family in a deprived area. Her mother lives on benefits, suffers from asthma and has had multiple partners. Debbie's own life and relationships are unpredictable and volatile. She is abusive (her brother, her mother) but may well have suffered abuse at an earlier stage of her life. At home, family members experience varying levels of distress and violence. Debbie has a reservoir of anger that erupts when teachers reprimand her. She has grown out of school and longs to leave. Her stance is profoundly disruptive.

Danièle lives in a near-derelict street where most of the houses are boarded up. Her mother lives on benefits and has no idea how to contain or manage her daughter, whose violence makes her a serious danger to other children. Although she is only 12 years old, Danièle is beyond the reach of mainstream schools and teachers. Chris Moore permanently excluded her on grounds of health and safety, but the LA was unable to provide an alternative placement. These are exceptional stories but they are of a type familiar for teachers who serve in ordinary comprehensives in Britain. Current policies do not acknowledge the impact of family and emotional difficulties on learning and teaching.

Diane Reay is concerned with a related problem, created by systems that produce teachers 'who learn nothing on their courses about how social class impacts on children's learning, let alone how to tackle the inequalities it generates' (Reay and de Waal, 2009:45). Successful students from disadvantaged backgrounds often struggle to overcome the social and cultural constraints of their early lives. Even those with outstanding academic results, whose later careers seem to confirm the role of education in social mobility, pay an emotional price for their success. Elena, a distinguished woman academic, remembers that she took a teaching post in the tough working class neighbourhood where she grew up. One of the parents recognised her and shouted in recognition:

> All the teachers heard – they couldn't believe that somebody from part of their group was working class – and the parents couldn't believe that the teacher was part of their working class group. I was stuck in the middle! And that's when I knew ... I knew I could not only never go back, but I would never be fully accepted in either camp. (Hoskins, 2010:17)

Elena's story shows the continuing emotional inhibitions that affect those whose intellectual ability leads them towards an improved social niche. Her youthful class identity and status were at variance with her later academic achievements and have been fractured by her success as an educator from a working class background. Her inherited 'theory-in-use' has proved inappropriate for the conditions in which she now lives. Elena's intense intellectual excitement has carried her through but many able working class children are inhibited at one stage or another by their perception of the social and emotional cost involved in acquiring a changed identity.

Policy-makers need to understand the price of success and to acknowledge that if 'the culture of the teacher is to become part of the consciousness of the child, then the culture of the child must first be in the consciousness of the teacher' (Basil Bernstein, quoted in Reay and de Waal, 2009:45). Whatever their ability, students are more likely to gravitate towards niches inhabited by people they perceive to be like themselves. Lateral movement between niches is more common than upward migration to unfamiliar social environments.

Other social, cultural and family constraints are less visible and less obviously disruptive. Small disadvantages accumulate and exert their influence below the smooth surface of school routines. The following student comments, however, when repeated singly or in combination, give telltale clues to mindsets that impede effective learning:

- I am not good enough – why bother when I can't win?
- I like to go out when I get home
- I've missed a lot of school with illness
- I am not like the posh kids who pass exams
- If I behave in class I get called a boff
- My dad didn't go to college – and he earns more than a teacher
- I'm unlucky
- I don't want a desk job
- Nobody cares about me
- I get respect by thumping geeks
- I help my mum at home because she can't cope on her own
- Teachers pick on me – I'm scared in lessons
- I like a smoke in the toilets and a laugh with my mates
- I don't like reading – the books are rubbish
- I've nowhere to work – my brother has music on all night.

No Hope of Improvement

Although the influence of geography, class and culture are well known, we persist with an individualist model of society, where people rise to the top through a combination of talent, education and hard work. Policy-makers disregard evidence that the slow evolution of social, cultural and family advantage is also necessary. Children stand on their parents' shoulders – they do not leap from nothing, dazzling everyone with stellar genius. Their later progress depends as well on practical intelligence and social and emotional resilience – some niche environments and status positions are potentially stressful or uncomfortable for those raised in humble circumstances.

This changed perspective exposes the naïve optimism of the school effectiveness story, where every teacher adds value, every student achieves high grades, and everyone climbs the social ladder. It also reveals the absurd paradox of school reform. If no child is left behind, no student can move ahead; if everyone has 5 good GCSE grades, employers must find some other way to distribute the limited supply of glittering and less glittering prizes. When we devise a means to enable gifted and talented students to rise despite unfavourable circumstances, their social mobility may change but cannot 'solve' the problems created by inequality and disadvantage. Competitive individualism promises opportunity and self-advancement but cannot reverse its own inherently unequal logic, however well educated we may all become. There are no individualist solutions to the problem of inequality, and no hope of serious improvement for the disadvantaged until a changed conception of success is adopted, and alternative measures of achievement are introduced.

3

Markets and Competition

Market Disciplines

Today's faith that competitive markets can stimulate schools to overcome disadvantage and so transform society is strong, despite the discomfort of market failure in 2008 and the evidence documented above. As the neo-liberal momentum became irresistible in the 1980s and 1990s, particularly after the collapse of the Soviet Union and its planned economy, English politicians rose above the 'old politics' to become technocrats, dedicated to easing the operation of free markets, especially in money and labour. After 2001, public sector reform became an urgent priority for New Labour. Ministers believed that commercial disciplines would transform the productivity, flexibility and quality of local services, including institutions such as schools, hospitals and prisons, and through them, increase the nation's human capital (Barker, 2009a).

The Blairite reform agenda has moved beyond the Conservative model of market-managerialism towards a hybrid, 'modernising' version of NPM. This combines market mechanisms with central control and regulation, including a pervasive audit and inspection apparatus. Power is dispersed through splits between policy and implementation, between purchasers and providers, and between the commissioning and delivery of services. This has fragmented the public services so there is continuous tension between control (e.g targets centrally prescribed and measured) and freedom (e.g local leadership and market choice). Public service markets are therefore very different from those defined by classical economists like Adam Smith. The government has intervened repeatedly to change the available offer of schools as well as the regulations shaping their operation (Cutler and Waine, 1997; Newman, 2001).

The 1988 Act created a quasi-market by reducing the extent to which LAs could control LMS and grant-maintained schools (GMS), and by introducing locally assessed admissions numbers for each school, so that preferences for particular schools could be denied only when the admission number had been reached. GM schools were also permitted to manage their own admissions and to select some students by aptitude or ability. Thirty per cent of schools now determine their own admissions, compared with 15 per cent in 1988. Since 1997, New Labour administrations have intensified the diversity of the market by creating new categories of school (faith schools, academies), by greatly expanding the number of specialist schools and colleges, and by extending the scope of competitive tendering for government contracts in educational services (West and Pennell, 2003; Gewirtz, 2002).

These local markets for nationally controlled products may seem contrived but the imagery of choice and entrepreneurial freedom suggests, nevertheless, a world where the culture of complacent workers and unions has been swept away in favour of managers who apply scientific techniques to ensure optimum results, with students driven to achievements that appear beyond them. In the mind's eye, the journey is from the over-manned and technically inefficient plants that produced the East German Trabant to the automated lines in the West that assembled the Mercedes Benz C-Class.

Stated in these terms, the claim that market disciplines create the best conditions for learning seems irresistible. We all have some experience of workplace cultures and practices that are poorly adjusted to client needs, and have suffered frustrating colleagues who have been less committed and determined than ourselves. The public and many politicians are disposed, like Julian Le Grand (2006), to doubt the altruism of public service 'knights' and to question whether some of the lazy, incompetent teachers they have met should be trusted to run the system. Even the quasi-markets in education, funded by the government rather than the customer, seem to offer the enticing prospect of improved motivation and sharper performance.

Despite the time, money and energy invested in creating and developing competitive markets in education, the innovation has failed, nevertheless, to deliver the expected improvements in quality and performance. This historic failure, comparable in its own way to the breakdown of the business model behind sub-prime mortgages, stems from the assumptions made by the 1988 policy-makers. Kenneth Baker (Conservative education secretary, 1986-1989) and his advisers were more concerned with ideological fashion than with an objective analysis of the problems of comprehensive schools (Simon, 1988). After 1989 and the collapse of Soviet communism in eastern Europe, leading neo-liberal politicians and thinkers began to believe they were witnessing the end of history and the consequent triumph of Western liberal democracy as the final form of government (Fukuyama, 1992). Free markets seemed to have become the ultimate arbiter of quality and value and would force inferior or unhealthy organisations to improve or disappear, like the motor industry in the German Democratic Republic.

As a result, the 1988 Act treated the comprehensives of the day as if they were more inclusive and more similar than was in reality the case, and underestimated the long-term impact of social class on children and schools. Self-help was the dominant strand in Conservative thought and obscured the history of oppression, struggle and injustice that had shaped English schooling. The impact of disadvantage on school provision and educational opportunity has to be understood before the failure of market competition can be explained.

Social Segregation
The English school system that emerged by the end of the nineteenth century was socially segregated, marked by tension and conflict, and complex in its structure and operation. The wealthy elite was served by an exclusive group of prestigious public schools; the prosperous middle class by endowed grammar schools of uneven quality; and the working and lower middle classes by elementary schools that had expanded rapidly in size and number to meet demand in the aftermath of the 1870 Education Act.

The variety of institutions within each of these broad categories reflected a diverse social geography and history, with some endowed schools achieving strong academic reputations while others struggled, and with the elementary sector divided between public and voluntary (church) provision. A small but significant number of co-educational higher grade elementary schools in urban areas retained older pupils beyond the official leaving age and entered them for the Science and Art Department examinations, so forging new coeducational opportunities and opening links with colleges of higher education (Vlaeminke, 1999).

The expansion of public education, especially in the cities, increased the tensions between social groups and stimulated competition between different types of school. In 1902, a Conservative government acted to remove the threat to established interests posed by new forms of education. The school boards that had promoted the apparently natural extension of the elementary system were abolished. Administrative measures were introduced that destroyed the higher grade schools themselves, and funds were provided for a highly selective model of secondary education that imitated the 'ethos' of the public schools. This intangible, prized feature of public and grammar schools seems to have been created through a strange mixture of the classics, rugby football, expensive uniforms and muscular Christianity. The demands of science, technology and industry were discounted, with incalculable consequences for the future (Barnett, 1986).

The 1902 Act has enjoyed an undeserved reputation for laying the foundations of secondary education in England. In reality, it crushed those schools that did provide opportunity for ordinary people, and failed to provide an adequate bridge between the elementary schools and secondary education. Less than 20 per cent of the maintained grammar school population was drawn from skilled manual backgrounds by 1913, while only two per cent came from unskilled families. Even by 1938, no more than 14 per cent of those eligible attended secondary schools (Kerckoff et al, 1996; Simon, 1999).

The 1944 Education Act, although influenced by R.H. Tawney's (1922) arguments in favour of 'secondary education for all', and promising a tripartite mix of grammar, technical and secondary modern schools, was in reality slow to increase the numbers participating in post-elementary courses. The school leaving age was not raised from 14 to 15 until 1947, and was not aligned with the requirements of the 16+ leaving examinations until 1972. This delay added to the generations of children who left school with no formal qualifications. In the 1950s and 1960s, few secondary moderns entered their pupils for General Certificate of Education (GCE) Ordinary (O) levels while Advanced (A) levels were accessible only to those who transferred to grammar schools.

The suppression of educational opportunity for the greater part of the population in 1902 was intentional and reflected the views of those who were troubled by the working class masses and frightened by their education. H.G. Wells regarded 'the extravagant swarm of new births' as 'the essential disaster of the nineteenth century'; while T.S. Eliot complained that 'our headlong rush to educate everyone' would lower standards and destroy 'our ancient edifices to make ready the ground upon which the barbarian nomads of the future will encamp their mechanised caravans.' Aldous Huxley disapproved of what he called 'universal education' because it had created 'an immense class of ... the New Stupid' (Wells, 1961:240; Eliot, 1968:185; Huxley, 1934:101).

Segregation (by social class), discrimination (against the masses) and slow progress (the times were parsimonious) are often written about as if they belonged to a distant era, separated from our own by a long period of scientific enlightenment and without relevance for our present problems. Unfortunately, the consequences of past attitudes and policies are significant for our own time. The post-war baby-boomer generation was brought up in a divided school system that limited sixth form opportunities to about 20 per cent of the population and university education to less than 4 per cent. Their parents were fortunate indeed if they received anything but an elementary education. Their grandparents were mainly the products of local and voluntary arrangements that barely constituted a system at all.

The wasted talent and lost opportunities of the first half of the twentieth century are almost unbearable to contemplate but education reformers find it convenient now to forget the history of state sponsored injustice, and to blame instead the schools and teachers who failed to reverse the waves of waste and loss. When comprehensives began to repair the damage, they were swiftly condemned for the long history of disadvantage they inherited. School reform is based on a massive ignorance of history that allows politicians and their advisers to convince themselves that the world began in 1988, with every school and child granted similar capacities and opportunities, and equally equipped to compete in a devil-take-the-hindmost market.

Educational Histories

My grandfather, Herbert Barker, born in 1879, and my father, Chris Barker, born in 1914, illustrate the educational disadvantage experienced by ordinary working people in the nineteenth century and in the first half of the twentieth. Herbert's mother died as a result of his birth and he found himself a virtual orphan. He was educated at the Derby Union (workhouse), where he is recorded as an inmate in the 1901 census. Intelligent, literate and energetic, he became a soldier, was commended for his service in caring for 17,000 men and horses during the South African war, and rose to the rank of warrant officer class 2. Back home in the Edwardian period he became a baker and confectioner in Peckham, and raised a family of four children, including my father.

During the Great War my grandfather served in India and then Mesopotamia. When the fighting was over he discovered, like other soldiers of that period, that Lloyd George was unable to keep his promise to build 'Homes Fit for Heroes'. As a result, the six members of the Barker family and grandmother Elizabeth moved to a privately rented, three bedroom house at 9 Hartnoll Street, London N7 that was part of a slum, cleared in the 1920s. Domestic arrangements were primitive. Grandfather Herbert now became a postman in Holloway, while son Chris was sent to Drayton Park elementary school where he studied from 1919 to 1927. His memoir, written for his granddaughter, records that at age 7 he advanced from the infant section to the 'Big Boys', as the elementary school was known. He remembered sticks of chalk thrown across a very large, partitioned classroom and reported learning algebra in the year before he left. Mr. Hayward, the English teacher, memorably explained that nouns name, and adjectives describe (Barker, 2002).

Chris's leaving certificate, dated 26th January 1928 and signed by a new headmaster, Mr. Palmer, declared that he:

> attended ... for eight years, leaving at Christmas 1927. He was a thoroughly reliable boy, honest and truthful, and a splendid worker. His conduct throughout was excellent: he was one of the school prefects and carried out his duties well. He was very intelligent.

So ended his formal education. He had shown himself to be 'very intelligent' and 'a splendid worker', so it was obvious that he had no need for secondary education and would be well adapted to the task of delivering messages in the Post Office's money order department.

My father told me that no boy from Drayton Park ever won a London County Council scholarship to grammar school. I do not know whether this is factually true but it was his impression of the opportunities available to him and to his family. Writing home in 1945, Chris described washing up in the officers' mess in Naples, and complained that without a proper education his natural eloquence and writing ability were of no avail. He was in charge of the education hut, but felt he should have been lecturing on the trade union and cooperative movement for the Army Bureau of Current Affairs. Later, he progressed by seniority through the ranks of the London Post Office, finally becoming an assistant superintendent.

Alan North[6] (pseudonym), who became vice chancellor of a large and distinguished university in the 1990s, provides a contrasting example of the workings of the English education system. Born before World War II, Alan grew up as the eldest of four children, crowded into a small two bedroom terraced house. His father was an agricultural labourer who later became a shift worker at a local power plant, while his mother was an unqualified nursing assistant. Neither parent received secondary education.

Their home had no bathroom, no indoor toilet and no hot water. The water closet was at the bottom of the garden. Gaslight was available only on the ground floor. A black lead grate in the front room provided the only heating. The slaughterhouse stood on one side of the road and the public house on the other. Alan and his two brothers would play football outside on a cinder patch while his sister joined in with other girls on the street, enjoying games with a skipping rope. On a Saturday, the youngsters would follow one another into a large tin bathtub for the weekly wash. Although the children wore hand-me-down clothes, Alan remembers they always had plenty to read. At the age of 8 he would go with one of his brothers to the library, returning with armfuls of more or less adult books, including westerns for himself and detective stories for his mother.

As their mother was a strong Methodist, the children went to Sunday School from an early age and enjoyed little entertainments and discussion as well as the religious element. Alan says the local primary school was fantastic. When he was only 10 years old a young woman teacher arranged for him to audition for the BBC Children's Hour in Manchester. After that, she encouraged him to sing and to read more demanding books. On a Friday afternoon she would get him to read to the class or even tell a story of his own. The war came and Alan remembers a large shell coming through the roof of the house opposite, only twenty yards away, and also observing aerial dogfights over the river estuary at the bottom of the hill. All the children were evacuated in 1940. He cannot recollect having any schooling during the year he was away.

Despite this interrupted education, he passed the 11+ and transferred to the only grammar school in town, housed in an old building criticised by inspectors in their 1908 report. The school was unusual in taking boys and girls. There were places for about two thirds of the top class from his local primary. Alan found his new place a 'big new world' with blazers, gowns and strict discipline but soon began to enjoy playing cricket and football and being taught by older male teachers who were returning from the war. Alan was in the fourth year when everyone moved three miles down the road to new premises, built before the war but requisitioned by the Ministry of Supply until 1948. The pupils were divided between the County School for Girls and the County School for Boys. Alan became school captain for soccer and cricket but his teachers complained that he was not doing himself justice with his academic work.

He describes his best teachers as 'genuine academics' who drove him to extend himself. He fell in love with French literature and could not read enough poetry and novels. The history teacher invited the boys to garden parties at his house; the Latin master gave him private lessons. In the sixth form he studied English, French, Latin and History and achieved As and Bs in his School Certificate examinations. Alan regards himself as having been lucky with his parents, schools and teachers, in both primary and grammar schools. But he also began to realise that he was losing his working class identity and culture. He sensed he 'was being changed' and was unsure how he felt about it. His mother was anxious too, remarking to his brother 'I hope Alan knows where he belongs'. The momentum of his academic interests carried him forward nevertheless. He won a place at university to study languages and philosophy, and eventually surprised himself by achieving a 1st class degree. His mother 'knew it was something great because people told her it was'. After university, he became a 2nd lieutenant in the army and led anti-terrorist operations against the Malayan insurgency, before embarking on a career as a teacher and academic. The County Grammar Schools were reorganised in 1978 and the resulting co-educational comprehensive has continued to enjoy a strong local reputation.

Dilemmas and Consequences

These reconstructed, subjective biographies of three working class males[7], born in 1879, 1914 and 1934 respectively, illustrate the intrinsic injustice of educational provision in the late Victorian period and the early twentieth century. They also suggest the dilemmas involved in extending opportunities for education, so that the absolute number of properly educated employees was adequate for national needs, and so that talented individuals could rise from the ranks to positions where they could contribute to the quality and efficiency of national life. The biographies have a further value in indicating the personal and emotional consequences of failure and success for the individuals concerned.

There is substantial evidence that my grandfather and father possessed great energy and ability. Herbert survived the workhouse to distinguish himself in the army and had the organisational skills to manage 17,000 men and horses. He learned to be a cook and in civilian life supported a growing family from his work as a baker and confectioner. After the Great War he secured a non-manual job as a postman. Chris's energy and verbal skills were recognised at school and he became a distinguished journalist, writing hundreds of articles for Post Office publications, from 1932 to 2004. Although he always described himself as working class, he ended his career in charge of London Chief Office and lived for 58 years in the semi-detached house he bought with his wife in 1947, using their combined war savings.

The Derby workhouse ensured Herbert's survival and basic education. Chris's success at age 16 in securing a high place in the Post Office general examination, and his well written articles, show that Drayton

Park provided him with a strong if elementary grounding in reading, writing and arithmetic. Despite their energy, determination and general ability, however, neither my father nor grandfather was considered suitable for secondary education. They were denied access to literature, poetry, art, drama, music, science and languages. They never met teachers who invited them to their houses or encouraged them to develop academic interests. The 1902 Act closed an iron door on successive generations of ordinary people by making sure that no elementary school was in a position to respond to the needs of talented pupils or the aspirations of their parents.

Herbert and his youngest son were not passive or unconscious victims of this regime. Both were supporters of the Labour Party and understood how class and privilege shaped their lives. Unlike his father, Chris was involved in active trade unionism, campaigned for equal rights for women clerks and supported the Republican government in Spain. He continued his education through summer schools, the newspapers and adult classes, so developing a deep political understanding that reflected the views of the moderate left during the 1930s. He knew that he hadn't been educated properly and understood the consequences of his lack of formal qualifications. Although he was not ambitious in career terms, he was less than keen to wash-up for the middle classes and remained a vigorous supporter of left-wing causes all his life. Learning from his own experience, he was passionate about education and sent both his sons to a London comprehensive.

These fragments of family history are consistent with our knowledge of social injustice in this period but they also provide evidence of another, less well-known story of social progress that unfolded despite the rigid and limiting structures of education at that time. The Barkers were intelligent enough and educated enough to benefit from a dramatic increase in non-manual and middle class employment from 20.3 per cent in 1911 to 30.4 per cent by 1951. Economic growth in the 1930s prompted the expanding middle class, including members of the Barker family, to purchase suburban semi-detached villas that 'became manifestations of their new property-owning status' and symbolised their remoteness from 'any image of poverty in which many had grown up' (Oliver *et al*, 1981:14). My father's education may have lagged behind his ability and aspirations but a good elementary education and public sector employment were invaluable advantages at a time when few people had obtained formal qualifications of any kind.

Alan North's very different and later story captures the beginning of the modern era, when serious efforts were made to expand the supply of educated people to match the changed employment conditions of the 1930s and 1940s. He was amongst the early achievers from working class backgrounds who won academic honours against the odds, and his educational history reveals some of the dilemmas faced by administrators responsible for easing the grip of the inflexible 1902 settlement.

This was a period of scarce resources, when even the economist John Maynard Keynes was uncertain whether public sector interventions could counter the downside of the business cycle. Existing secondary schools were relatively small, with little spare capacity, and the capital available for new buildings was limited. The number of scholarships to support those who could not afford secondary school fees could be increased, but not so quickly that the supply of funds and places was exhausted. The result was that talented children found opportunities for upward mobility, while the majority was contained within the bounds of the unsatisfactory elementary system left behind by 1902.

The number of scholarship places at secondary schools increased slowly between 1925 (Chris Barker age 11) and 1945 (Alan North age 11) and there were progressively better opportunities for talented girls and boys in the post-war years. The 1944 Education Act established the principle that secondary education should be free to all, rather than dependent on scholarships, but the number of selective places continued to be limited and subject to local variation. In some LAs as many as 40 per cent of a cohort might be offered places; in others only 18 per cent were deemed academic. The post-war building programme, especially in places like London, Leicestershire and Hertfordshire, created new and better secondary opportunities for everyone, and experiments with multi-lateral and all-ability schools were also helpful in shaping a broader-based and more just education system.

Alan experienced an improvised version of mass education based on adopting the meritocratic principle for a small but significant minority of children, and with his family pioneered some of the dilemmas and tensions associated with selection and upward social mobility. In a curious way, because so few pupils were awarded scholarships, elementary schools served the whole of the community in which they were located. With the growth of intelligence testing and the 11+ system in the 1930s and 1940s, working class children who passed the exam found themselves leaving their friends, families and native culture behind and were often burdened with feelings of alienation and guilt. Alan's mother hoped he would remember where he belonged and he was himself disturbed by the ways in which academic education changed his interests and perhaps his very being. Like many working class parents in the years to come, Alan's parents were proud but troubled as their son embarked on a strange and incomprehensible new life that took him away from them, in terms of income, location and culture. His ability removed him from the community to which he belonged and whose interests he wished to advance.

Working Class Emancipation

Alan's story seems also to validate the proposition that in those halcyon days immediately before and after the second world war, grammar schools offered a distinctive ethos and academic excellence that enabled students like him to escape humble origins and tangible poverty. It also encourages the popular prejudice that such splendid institutions should never have been merged into comprehensives during the great reorganisation of the 1960s and 1970s. Alan continues to be enthusiastic about his old school and the world it opened for him.

Recent nostalgia for a lost social order may be understandable but depends on cheerful ignorance of educational reality at the time. Alan North grew up in a hyper-selective system that guaranteed every grammar school an intake of exceptionally gifted children. In such favourable conditions, beyond the dreams of the comprehensive schools to come, it should have been impossible to fail. Even so, grammar schools often did fail their working class pupils. In Huddersfield, for example, 64 per cent of the grammar school students who passed A level in the immediate post-war period had middle class fathers, while only 36 per cent had working class fathers. The balance between the two classes in the city population was almost reversed in the grammar schools. The percentage of middle class girls who passed their A levels at Ash Grange actually increased from 68 per cent (in the period 1949-1951) to 74 per cent (in the period 1952-1954), and confirmed evidence from other sources that the 1944 Education Act had little impact on the performance gap between the classes (Jackson and Marsden, 1986).

Brian Jackson and Dennis Marsden used these figures to argue that there was a 'colossal waste of talent in working-class children' (1986, p16). Pupils from working class backgrounds were less likely to be selected for grammar schools; were less likely to do well in public examinations; and were less likely to progress to higher education. The Crowther Report (1959) found that 75 per cent of middle class entrants to National Service had some form of selective education, mainly in grammar schools, while 85 per cent of working class recruits had attended secondary moderns. The *Early Leaving Report* (Ministry of Education, 1954) noted that children from semi-skilled and unskilled backgrounds obtained only half as many grammar school places as might be expected. This data relates to a period when the working class accounted for 75 per cent of the adult population.

Some exceptionally gifted working class students, like Alan North, passed the 11+ and were given educational opportunities that had not been available in the previous generation. But the system as a whole rationed these new opportunities and worked in ways that favoured middle class families. It is absurd to praise the grammar schools of this period as agents of social emancipation when we know that the vast majority of working class children were sent to secondary moderns as remote from sixth forms and higher education as the old elementary schools had been.

In the 1960s Jackson and Marsden (1986) were convinced that if education could be opened as freely to working-class children as it had been for middle-class ones, society's highly talented and educated groups could be doubled and doubled again. As we know now, this was a serious under-estimate of the number of students who had the ability to benefit from secondary and higher education, but at that time many observers argued that the small proportion of children admitted to grammar schools had already exhausted the supply of suitable talent.

Comprehensive Education

Brian Jackson and Dennis Marsden were Alan North's contemporaries and progressed as he did from working class backgrounds to higher education. Like him, they experienced the strangeness of grammar school and university culture and tried hard to understand the impact on their own identities. After returning to Huddersfield to research working class families, they concluded that the whole system of selection was wrong and discriminated against working class people and their culture. They argued for a new type of democratic education:

> The educational system we need is one which accepts and develops the best qualities of working-class living ... Before this can begin we must put completely aside any early attempts to select and reject in order to rear an elite ... We must firmly accept the life of the majority and be bold and flexible in developing new forms – the open school which belongs to the neighbourhood, the open university which involves itself in local life rather than dominates or defies it. (Jackson and Marsden, 1986:10)

Education and the Working Class (Jackson and Marsden, 1986) contributed to a growing consensus that selection at 11+ was premature, unfair and wasteful and that comprehensives would offer greater fairness and opportunity. Early experiments with more inclusive types of school encouraged faith in all-ability models of education, while the post-war baby boom created an acute demand for accommodation. New, large, coeducational comprehensives seemed to offer the most economical and publicly acceptable solution to the pressures that were building. David Eccles, Conservative Minister of Education, warned the cabinet in 1955 that the 11+ had become a critical political issue. Aspiring parents were increasingly angry when their children were labelled as failures and their frustrations were expressed in a broad-based social movement that demanded a fair education system (Simon, 1991).

By 1963 the country no longer believed it could afford to place a small minority of children in elite grammar schools, and leave up to 80 per cent of the population in secondary moderns that provided a limited curriculum for 11 to 15 year olds, with few realistic routes into sixth forms and beyond. The 1950s and 1960s were shaped by the post-war welfare settlement, when the equilibrium between competing interests was in favour of Keynesian economics, distributive justice, respect for enlightened public administration, and trust in professional expertise (Clarke and Newman, 1997: Gewirtz, 2002).

The dispersed, grass roots nature of the movement for comprehensive education was its strength and weakness. Some LAs were swift to respond to new problems and conditions, others gradually accepted government prompts to reorganise their schools on comprehensive lines, while a small minority (e.g Kent, Lincolnshire) were stubbornly resistant to the spirit of the times and have retained the 11+ to this day. A few enlightened LAs (e.g Leicestershire, Buckinghamshire, Cambridgeshire) created new community schools that aimed to provide for families and children throughout their lives.

The tensions and conflicts between social groups were played out at local level, producing a complex, variegated pattern that included many interpretations of all-ability schooling. LA policies were shaped by history and geography as well as contests between political parties and ideologies. Despite these constraints, considerable progress was made during the 1960s and 1970s towards a national system that was comprehensive, and gave students fair access to educational opportunities (Benn and Chitty, 1996).

The early comprehensives often operated in challenging conditions, with many able children creamed into the local grammar schools that continued to operate. This was true even where political support for the comprehensive principle was strong. Eltham Green School, for example, opened in south London in 1956, with accommodation for a total of 1950 pupils and a sixth form. A girls' grammar school successfully resisted incorporation in the new school, and other local grammars were within easy reach by bus. This led to unfair competition and an Eltham Green intake biased towards boys (by 2 to 1) and lower ability groups. Between 1958 and 1962, the school continued to receive a quota of able pupils that was 10 per cent of the total rather than the expected 20 per cent. In this same period, the school was consistently under-subscribed in terms of first choice applications, so that up to 50 per cent of the intake came from outside the neighbourhood (Eltham Green, 1963).

Similar difficulties were reproduced across the country as an *ad hoc* network of new comprehensives struggled through the 1970s and 1980s to establish academic credentials and good reputations. Traditional patterns of schooling were disrupted everywhere, although comprehensive reorganisation proceeded gradually and with local consent. People who regarded the grammar school as an exclusive symbol of their own status and identity tended to perceive the new social democratic order in education as a threat to be resisted or escaped. They agreed with the Black Papers[8] and believed the lurid stories of disorder that appeared in the popular press.

As social groups manoeuvred for advantage within a rapidly changing configuration of schools, flexible hierarchies based on folk memory and reputation replaced the well-defined boundaries of the selective system. Local social structures began to adapt to the patchwork of inclusive schools that had emerged, with many families manoeuvring to buy homes near schools perceived to be more successful and desirable than others (Ball, 2003a). LAs attempted to manage intakes to achieve a degree of equity, but with mixed results (Cox and Dyson, 1969; Simon, 1991).

Markets in Education

The education market introduced after 1988 was designed to resolve the social tensions, ideological controversies and quality concerns that had developed around the fledgling comprehensive system. The four main aims were:

- To create choice for parents frustrated by controlled access to popular schools
- To increase equity by opening good schools to students from every part of town, not just from a privileged catchment area
- To give managers and parents freedom to enhance their well-being and improve individual motivation and performance
- To encourage competition between schools that would lead to improved quality and outcomes.

Despite their roots in neo-liberal ideology, these are honourable, perhaps desirable goals. Unfortunately, key policy assumptions immediately compromised the effectiveness of the new markets. Ministers believed that schools had an equal chance of success, provided they responded competitively to the businesslike environment that had been created. They were also convinced that heads and their teachers were fully responsible for educational outcomes and for the marked differences between schools observed by critics. Finally, policy-makers failed to recognise that the regulatory regime established in 1988 would undermine the freedoms that were supposed to liberate managers from LA bureaucracy. In time these key assumptions undermined progress towards each of the policy aims identified above.

Creating Choice

By removing LAs' right to manage pupil intakes, open enrolment was supposed to eliminate the main obstacle to choice and to create a fair competition for pupils between schools in a given location. Unfortunately the supply of places was relatively inflexible, and not easily adjusted to fluctuations in demand. There is limited scope, therefore, to accommodate the imbalances between over- and under-subscribed schools, and between advantaged and disadvantaged areas. This means that some schools are in a position to choose their students, while others reach their admission limits only by accepting children disappointed elsewhere. LAs are under pressure to reduce costs by removing surplus places but also face the dilemma that the most unpopular schools continue to recruit more pupils than can be accommodated at accessible alternatives. The more efficient provision becomes, the harder it is to close a school that accommodates substantial numbers.

Although the 1988 legislation aimed to weaken the link between a student's place of residence and school attended, and so to encourage mobility, children living outside the catchment area of an over-subscribed school find it difficult to secure places there. The scope for choice is less than it seems, so that many parents are no less frustrated today than they were in 1988. In some LAs the pressure on popular schools is now so great there is talk of using lotteries to reduce the effect of social segregation.

Increasing Equity

There is abundant evidence that far from increasing equity, the operation of the market has reversed the trend towards more equal opportunities established in the years before the 1988 Education Act. The most important influence here is that the quasi-market has been engineered so that some schools and children are more favoured than others. Successive governments have created new types of school (e.g City Technology Colleges, Grant-Maintained/Foundation[9] Schools,

Specialist Colleges, Academies, Faith Schools) that have received a variety of incentives and benefits, including additional funds, better buildings and the right to select part of their intake by ability. This has enabled a significant minority of voluntary aided (i.e church) and Foundation schools to use admissions criteria that have an exclusive or selective effect, including those relating to aptitude, ability banding and religious commitment. Ministers and officials have defended their interventions as increasing diversity but this begs the question of whether it is the government or market competition that is determining the available choice of school (West *et al*, 2004).

Some groups are more adept than others at negotiating the patchwork provision that has developed from these initiatives. Families from lower socio-economic backgrounds seem to be disadvantaged in their ability to access supposedly better schools. They may lack the time, money and information to exercise effective choice, or they may be trapped on an estate by their personal circumstances. Alternatively, working class people may not feel comfortable with the ethos and values associated with what they perceive as middle class education, and they may identify strongly with a particular community and be content with their local school, even if the examination results are not particularly impressive (Allen, 2007; Gewirtz *et al*, 1995; Ball, 2003a).

Middle class families tend to adopt a variety of strategies to secure the right placement for their children, and to value those schools that recruit students with higher ability and socio-economic status. Middle class parents seek out information, talk to gatekeepers, and work out a variety of plans to get their children into a small number of schools. They are prepared to move home and assiduously select what they see as appropriate schools that match the perceived characteristics of their individual child (Gewirtz *et al*, 1995; Ball, 2003a; Butler *et al*, 2007).

The consequences of these manoeuvres are predictable and reveal the gross imperfections of the quasi-market that has operated since 1988. Intakes have become more polarised, with very successful schools recruiting from a wide area, and with the less successful obliged to draw from a narrowly defined location. When pupils move away from the schools nearest their homes, social and ability segregation are increased. The imposed structure of the market, the rules governing its operation, and the response of families and children to the available choices have all reduced equity (Allen, 2007; Butler *et al*, 2007).

Increasing Freedom

Parents were supposed to be empowered by the opportunity to exercise choice and to take responsibility for their children's future. The leaders of self-managing (LMS) and self-governing (GMS) schools were supposed to become entrepreneurs, motivated by their new managerial freedoms. These hopes are hard to reconcile with the limited choice that has been available and the intensely managed and controlled nature of the market.

Parents are free to choose schools for their children but their individual choices risk the disruption of the communities to which they belong. School leaders have acquired chequebooks, budgets and additional responsibilities for personnel management, but they have lost control and engagement with the curriculum and with assessment. They are subjected to a coercive style of inspection and audit that does not encourage innovation or a climate of creative freedom. The pervasive authority of the bureaucratic state and its agents remains strong. The Thatcherite critique of the deadening influence of the government apparatus seems no less valid today than it was in the years leading up to the 1988 legislation.

Encouraging Competition

A causal connection between competition and quality has not been demonstrated in medicine and education, mainly because learning and health are not products or commodities to be mass-produced but states of mind and being to which patients and students contribute far more than the facilities they use. The publication of surgical success indicators or GCSE results, for example, may reveal as much about the neighbourhood in which institutions are based as the schools and hospitals themselves.

The performance tables, based on unadjusted statistics, tell the reader more about a school's social composition and intake than its quality as an organisation, and create unjustified reputations that encourage ambitious families to move their children from less to more prosperous neighbourhoods and schools. The drive for excellence at a particular school may produce, therefore, a virtuous circle where a better intake attracts more able teachers and results improve. The trouble is that a progressive redistribution of students and teachers within a local hierarchy of schools has uncertain long-term consequences, and is unlikely to produce a general benefit for the wider community. There is no evidence that competitive pressures have improved teaching methods or have stimulated innovation and creativity. On the contrary, the hyper-accountability system has encouraged compliance and convergence (Levačić and Woods, 2002a, 2002b; Lupton, 2004).

Consequences

Choice, diversity and competition have multiplied the inequities of English education, therefore, and have reversed the progress achieved by comprehensive schools in the aftermath of reorganisation in the 1970s and 1980s. The differences between schools have been increased rather than reduced, while new and divisive types of school have been created, so that the system is more polarised and less fair than before. The mechanisms of choice have produced patterns of schooling that weaken neighbourhood communities and increase existing social divisions.

The ideology of markets has been disastrous for policy because it has driven Ministers to concentrate on an approach to education provision that has proved particularly unhelpful and unproductive. Despite talk of social inclusion, no serious attempt has been made to deal with the consequences of a long history of educational disadvantage charted in this chapter and with the complex problems associated with ensuring equitable provision. In the circumstances, is not surprising that relative poverty continues to be a major problem.

4

Imagine an End to Failure

Reforming Schools

Although markets were expected to improve performance and raise standards, policy-makers were also eager to deal with the deep endemic failures of the education system and to ensure that sick or failing schools were swiftly restored to health. In his *TES/Greenwich* lecture, Sir Michael Barber (1995) presented his imagined end to school failure. He estimated that by the time Ofsted had completed its four-year cycle, there would be between 250 and 500 failing schools in the country. Between 1,500 and 2,500 further schools would be identified as having serious weaknesses. He challenged the assumption that many disadvantaged schools and children must inevitably fail and argued for government intervention to increase the reliability of the education system. A 90 per cent success rate is unacceptable for air traffic control – so why is it tolerable in education?

Through Ofsted, the Conservative government already aimed to identify and improve failing schools. Officials at the DfEE believed the public naming of struggling schools was a success:

> By January 1997, well over 250 schools had been through this shock. Ofsted and DfEE, having worked closely with each school, are perhaps best placed to reach an overall judgement. It is our joint conclusion that the public identification of unacceptable standards tends to speed rather than delay recovery, and indeed is often a precondition for it. (Stark, 1998:35)

The solutions were straightforward. Weak schools needed to deal with serious breakdowns in leadership, face up to failure, prepare an action plan, improve standards and 'embark on the third stage, progression towards excellence' (Stark, 1998:36).

After New Labour's election victory in May 1997, David Blunkett, Secretary State for Education, was determined to demonstrate the Blair government's 'zero tolerance of failure'. He said that 'difficult situations demand tough solutions' and published a list of eighteen schools believed to be unsatisfactory for a variety of reasons (Baker, 2008). Michael Barber became head of the Standards and Effectiveness Unit (SEU) and was ruthless in mobilising the power of the state to deal with perceived failure. The SEU, Ofsted, LAs and other government agencies were co-ordinated to enforce a performance regime based on demanding statistical targets. Schools that failed to match expectations were threatened with Ofsted categories (e.g special measures and serious weaknesses). Ceaseless initiatives (e.g Fresh Start, City Academies) included the ultimate threat of closure for those who improved their results too slowly.

Fourteen years later, however, there is little sign that a plethora of vigorous reform efforts have brought an end to failure or have reduced the number of 'failing' and 'struggling' schools. Wintour and Curtis (2008) report that:

> Ed Balls, the schools secretary, will reveal today that up to 270 schools will be closed in the next three years for underperformance and replaced with academies and a new generation of trust schools. Balls will unveil substantial plans today to drive up standards in the 638 schools identified as seriously underperforming, offering local authorities the option to provide intensive support to the schools or replace them with academies and schools supported by businesses, charities and other education institutions. He said he expected, on the basis of analysis of persistently underperforming schools that about 200 of the 638 will not improve fast enough and will be replaced by academies.

Undismayed by their slow progress so far, Ministers remain determined to end failure and to ensure that the conditions for high quality learning and teaching are accessible to all children. Academies are seen as a new and important part of a wider programme of public service reform, intended to promote choice, diversity and personalised provision in education (Adonis, 2008). They are also designed to end a long history of perceived school failure in areas of acute social disadvantage. Although the government's unrelenting optimism is in many ways admirable, there are dangers in embarking on a further wave of reform without properly understanding why previous efforts to transform education have been so unsuccessful.

My own recent involvement with St Michael's Church School[10] in the East Midlands provides the data for a case study designed to explore the local impact of top down reform. Government agencies have worked on St. Michael's for a period of over five years and their lack of success demonstrates fundamental flaws in Barber's conception of school reform and improvement (Barber, 1995).

St. Michael's was placed in special measures in February 2008. The school was fast-tracked to become an academy in November 2008. The imbroglio that followed provides an opportunity to evaluate the apparatus of recent public sector reform, and to understand the problems faced by governmental agencies as they seek to create the conditions for high quality learning.

Implementing the Academy Programme:
A Case Study

I was watching television one evening when the telephone rang. I'm not at my best in these circumstances and have been known to swear and shout with indignation at interruptions. My wife says that she hates the smarmy way I speak once the handset is against my ear.

'Is that Bernard Barker?' asked an unfamiliar male voice.

'Yeah, that's me,' I replied, preparing to dismiss an intrusive marketing call.

'I've been given your name by Jon Grant. You used to work in Leicester,' he said.

I was caught. After a few months retired at home with nothing to do but travel, I smelt the scent of smoking guns and heard the shouts of battle. Over ten years ago I was in charge of a school in Leicester, determined to rescue it from special measures and closure, and Jon Grant was part of the parents' campaign that really saved the place. He was a smart guy and together we fought and won a good war.

'My name's Dennis Matthews,' said the caller, 'I hope you don't mind me contacting you so late.'

'No, no!' I answered in that voice my wife's told me about.

'Jon said give you a bell,' continued Dennis, 'He reckons you like a scrap.'

Dennis told his story. He has a son and daughter at St. Michael's Church School in Thornton in the East Midlands. They were doing fine with the new headteacher, Isobel Allen, until the government's standards juggernaut steamed in. Now the school is being fast-tracked to become an academy, with government ministers, the Diocese, the LA and Ofsted all conspiring to ride roughshod over the parents and children, who want to give Isobel a chance. DCSF is hell-bent on closure and plans to open a Church Academy in the same buildings. The Church sponsors have already appointed the principal-designate, a woman who left her previous job in suspicious circumstances after only ten months in post.

'What do Ofsted say?' I asked. Even governments have their reasons.

'We got a 'Notice to Improve' three years ago. Precious little was done about it,' answered Dennis. 'Ten months back they dumped us in special measures. Ofsted said the head and governors weren't capable of doing the job. It wasn't rocket science finding that out. Meddling, inept Diocese, laidback LA, hopeless head, massive budget deficit, unfinished buildings, big teacher turnover, millions of kids arriving on the doorstep with very little English, poor GCSE results. It was dire, Bernard, dire.'

'So what happened?'

'The old head was squeezed out.'

'By the governors?'

'No. By David Slope, director of education for the Diocese. He made her an offer she couldn't refuse.'

'And is that where Isobel Allen came in?'

'She was appointed last February, a week or two before the inspection that put us in special measures. Slope convinced her she would have the governors' full backing to sort the school out. She's told me what he said, 'budget first, then the useless teachers'. But all the time, he was talking to government advisers about making St. Michael's an academy, with the Diocese as lead sponsor.'

'What happens about Isobel if the academy goes ahead?'

'She's stuffed. But we think she's great, a really tough cookie who knows what she's doing and where she's going. The kids come home and they're buzzing about school. That's never happened before at St Michael's, not once since the wretched half-cock merger that brought the place into being.'

'OK, Dennis, so the academy plan gives the lunatics control of the asylum, have I got that right?' I asked to check my understanding.

'Absolutely. Exactly right Bernard. Do you want to help?'

For me this was an irresistible invitation. I don't like social injustice, especially when it is done to vulnerable teachers and children in disadvantaged areas. So I agreed to attend the LA's consultation meeting on the school's closure, due to be held at St. Michael's the following week. I told Dennis Matthews that I was not optimistic about the chances of stopping the academy because nowadays governments have the power to do more or less what they want. Local opinion doesn't really matter. He agreed. The DCSF had let it be known through the LA and Diocese that they were determined to go ahead and would take no prisoners. The school had consistently missed its targets and a Church Academy would bring new and better leadership as well as outside sponsorship.

One evening a week later, I travelled across the Midlands to Thornton, driving in the cold and steady rain to a tree-less neighbourhood of narrow streets that were lined by redbrick Victorian and Edwardian terraced houses. I juggled the steering wheel and my Google map in the darkness, unsure of where St Michael's would be. As I edged through the parked cars, I found the school, a cluster of two-storey, honey-coloured buildings set on high ground and skirted by security fencing. At the centre, linking two hall-like structures, was a plate glass atrium, blazing with light. Relieved, I drove through the gates, parked easily and found my way to the reception desk inside. An unusually cheerful caretaker directed me to the lecture theatre, where the consultation meeting was scheduled to start in about twenty minutes.

To reach the lecture theatre, I passed through a vast open space where volunteers were serving coffee to a handful of early arrivals. The walls were immensely high and broken by galleries that seemed to lead to classrooms but my initial impression was that I had somehow wandered inside an immense industrial warehouse or distribution centre, built of concrete and corrugated steel sheets. This measureless, unheated hall dwarfed the dining furniture set out in the central area, and reduced the parents and children within to Lowry-like figures, almost etched on the floor tiles. Dennis greeted me and explained that daily assemblies are held here, with over a thousand children and their teachers singing hymns and shivering in the cold.

He pushed through a pair of doors to the steeply raked lecture theatre where a scattering of parents and children had already taken their seats. A tall, smiling woman stood near the lectern, nodding graciously towards familiar faces. 'That's Janet Fitzpatrick,' he explained, 'LA Cabinet Member for education. She's unhappy with the way this has been handled so far. I think she knows the consultation has been bungled.'

Dennis was anxious that parents might not come in sufficient numbers. 'We need a big turnout tonight,' he said, 'We have to show we're serious.' He need not have worried. Shortly after 7.00 pm, the trickle of individuals through the double doors became a crowd as groups of parents and children climbed the steps to their seats, chattering amongst themselves and greeting their friends and fellow-campaigners as they went. 'It's a joke, the whole thing's a joke,' said a voice a few rows back. 'Bastards have made up their minds!' said another, audible throughout the theatre. Mrs. Fitzpatrick looked around, estimating the numbers that now filled most of the seats in the house. She smiled less easily as more and more eyes moved in her direction.

'I think we should start,' she said, leaning towards the microphone. 'This is your meeting...'

'Can't hear you!' shouted a voice at the back.

'This is your opportunity to...'

'Do you mind speaking up? We can't hear,' shouted a woman at the rear of the theatre, waving her arm and rising to her feet.

'Is that better?' said Mrs. Fitzpatrick, her words fading as she spoke.

'Switch it on!' shouted someone.

'The microphone isn't working,' bawled another.

Mrs. Fitzpatrick fumbled with a couple of switches on the lectern.

'Can you hear me now?'

Ironic applause confirmed that she could be heard.

'Well, thank you very much for coming to St. Michael's this evening. It is important for your voices to be heard...'

She was interrupted by further ironic applause.

'Now then, we all know St. Michael's hasn't been achieving the results we'd like...'

Protesting voices were heard.

'I'd like to begin by introducing tonight's panel,' she said, gesturing towards the front where a row of well-groomed suits nodded their uncomfortable approval of the proceedings.

'Representing the LA, we have Mr. Peter Slater, Director of Children's Services, and Alicia Arnold, School Improvement Adviser. Representing the Diocese and Sponsors, we have Archdeacon Dorothy Proud, Mrs. Charity Gooding, head-teacher of Bishop Grantly School in Barset, and last but not least, Dr. Tom Francis, principal of St. Saviour's College...'

'Where's that fellow Slope? Have you lost him?' asked an amused parent, half rising to interrupt.

'He's hiding,' shouted someone.

'We can't go on like this,' said Mrs. Fitzpatrick, shaking her head.

'Too darned right!' said Dennis.

'I'm running this meeting,' said Mrs. Fitzpatrick, 'I insist that you stand and give your names before speaking. Otherwise no one is heard.'

'I take exception to you running the meeting,' said a man in a suit, standing as he spoke.

'Your name!' demanded Mrs. Fitzpatrick.

'I'm Jim Perkins. I have a daughter in year 11 and a son in year 9,' continued the speaker, 'We've lived through this fiasco from the start and know what we're talking about. You said this is our meeting. Have you noticed no one here wants St. Michael's closed?'

'I don't think we've found that out yet,' said Mrs. Fitzpatrick.

'Then let's have a vote on it now,' said Jim, turning to survey the crowd, 'Hands up, everyone, all those in favour of closing the school.'

There was silence as people scanned the theatre. Not a hand moved.

'What did I tell you, not one vote,' said Jim.

Loud applause greeted the result.

'We'll do the voting at the end,' insisted Mrs. Fitzpatrick.

'No, let's do it now,' said Jim Perkins, 'Hands up those who want to keep it open!'

'This isn't acceptable,' protested Mrs. Fitzpatrick.

The theatre became a forest of waving hands.

'Do you want to count them?' asked Jim, 'I make it unanimous.'

Loud applause followed.

'What I want to ask about,' said a woman with a child near the front, 'Is the kids in year 6, what happens with them? We're completely in the dark.'

'That's an important point,' said Mrs. Fitzpatrick, 'Once the decision is made we'll get the information out to the primary schools.'

A large man with flowing grey hair struggled to his feet. 'I'm Richard Crick, and my boys are in years 8 and 10,' he said. 'Could you please tell us what options you've considered? What are the alternatives?'

'Alicia, I wonder if you could say a few words?' asked Mrs. Fitzpatrick, looking to the front row for help. Alicia Arnold rose in her seat, stepped forward and turned towards the audience.

'I think we have to look at the facts, Mrs. Fitzpatrick,' she said, her face partly obscured by long, thick hair. 'Very simply, St. Michael's is a school that isn't improving fast enough. In fact, it isn't improving at all. In its present format there isn't the capacity to improve. Attendance is not good enough; test and examination results are below the floor targets that have been set; and the value added figures are frankly poor.'

'Just a minute,' interrupted Richard Crick, 'We've heard all this before. You're not answering my question. I'm asking what alternatives were considered before the academy proposal was decided on.'

'As an authority, we've been working with the school to...' continued Alicia, with an air of great patience and sincerity.

'Not what Ofsted says,' interrupted a woman, thrusting a clutch of papers into the air and waving them enthusiastically. 'You've done sweet FA!'

'Your name, please!' called Mrs. Fitzpatrick, steadying herself on the lectern.

'I'm Doreen Blowers. They say you haven't reviewed or updated your action plan.'

'Hang on, hang on,' said Richard Crick, 'Are you going to answer my question or not?'

'That was the monitoring report before last,' said Alicia, turning towards Mrs. Blowers and adopting a long-suffering expression.

'Can we have one speaker at a time? I know you feel strongly but you must let people be heard,' said Mrs. Fitzpatrick.

'Could Mrs. Arnold answer me, please?' demanded Richard Crick. 'Were other options considered or did you just go for it?'

'Peter, I wonder if...'

Peter Slater, Director of Children's Services, stepped forward briskly and took his place beside Mrs. Fitzpatrick.

'I think I can help here, Madam Chairman,' he said, grasping the sides of the lectern in each hand. 'Last spring we met with the DCSF to discuss two basic options. These were to close the school or turn it into an academy. Closure was out of the question – we need the places in this part of town. When we looked at it, the solution was obvious, we needed something new, different, exciting, a scheme that would catch people's imagination.'

Richard Crick raised his hand. The Director stretched out an arm and gave way.

'You saw the vote. We're against it.'

'I'm afraid I must explain a very important point. The issue isn't a question of voting yes or no for the academy. The status quo isn't an option. We need to hear your views on the proposal. This is a consultation. But the status quo isn't an option. There's little evidence that the school can rise above the floor targets on its own initiative...'

'That's rubbish,' interjected Doreen Blowers, 'Ofsted say that Mrs. Allen is a strong leader with a sense of vision and direction.'

She turned over the pages on her lap. 'Here, look, 'strong leader' ... 'vision and direction' ... Why don't you let her get on with the job?'

There were shouts of approval, accompanied by vigorous applause.

'I'm afraid it isn't as simple as that,' said Peter Slater firmly when the noise subsided. 'The last monitoring report is clear, not enough progress has been made overall since the school was placed in Special Measures. We have to deal with that.'

'I'm Helen Lightfoot,' said a woman, 'And my boy Simon is in year 9. Where's the evidence that an academy will do the job? I think it's appalling, pulling the rug out from beneath the children's feet. Simon's been very quiet at home since all this has been going on. Mrs. Allen is the best thing that has happened here, ever. She's won the respect of the staff and children. And unlike your Mrs. Sparkler, Isobel Allen is a practising Christian!' (Mrs. Sparkler was the recently appointed principal-elect of the proposed academy)

The lecture theatre erupted with cheers, shouts and thunderous applause. Paul Slater's grip on the lectern tightened as his face reddened. Another mother stood up in the midst of the cheering and Mrs. Fitzpatrick nodded in her direction.

'I'm Martha Rainthorpe. My son Josh is in year 7. I've been reading the PricewaterhouseCoopers' Evaluation Report on Academies.'

She held up a copy of the document and coughed to clear her throat.

'Apparently,' she began, 'Academies don't come with a guarantee. Listen to this, on page 54.' She read from the Evaluation Report in a firm voice. 'In some academies, and depending on the indicator used, performance is actually deteriorating; in other academies, performance is improving in all subject areas, and in others, performance is improving in one subject and deteriorating in another.'

The other parents listened in hushed silence, as if the consultants' report had been elevated to the status of the Bible. 'Doesn't sound that good, does it Mr. Slater?' said Martha Rainthorpe, looking straight at the Director of Children's Services, who seemed, for the moment at least, uncertain how to reply. 'PricewaterhouseCoopers also say improvement is down to strong leadership. It's here on page 21.' She read from the PwC Report (2006):

> 'There is evidence that strong leadership is critical to the success of academies. For example, a significant number of pupils and parents in academies generally think highly of their principal and highlighted a number of positive areas including the principal's interest in and understanding of pupils' and parents' issues, their visibility around the school and their focus on fostering good behaviour.'

'Mrs. Fitzpatrick,' she continued, addressing the Cabinet Member directly. 'That's precisely what we've got already. We think Mrs. Allen is fantastic. She's an upfront leader and she's passionate about children and learning. What exactly are the benefits the academy will bring us? Do you know, or is the academy a leap in the dark?'

'We're left, nevertheless,' began Paul Slater, slightly flustered, 'with a simple fact. This is a failing school.'

'Why is it failing?' shouted someone.

'The evidence is set out in the Ofsted Report,' replied Paul Slater. 'Inconsistent teaching, with too many poor lessons; too much disruptive behaviour; a high exclusion rate; and very little improvement in the results.'

Dennis Matthews leapt to his feet.

'We also know why it failed, don't we! The guilty men and women are right there in the front row,' he shouted, pointing down to the Diocesan representatives, 'Inept bunglers who couldn't run a whelk stall! They meddled and fiddled but could they remove the old head? No way. The Diocesan director doesn't even have the guts to come here tonight and face the people he's screwed up.'

Amidst the applause and cheers, Helen Lightfoot began to speak again. 'Excuse me Councillor Fitzpatrick, could someone from the Diocese tell us why Isobel Allen didn't get the academy job? The way I understand it, Mrs. Allen started in September, with instructions from the governors to turn the school round. Two months later, the academy was proposed and the sponsors turned up without reference to the governors or consulting the parents and appointed a displaced head from London to take over next year. It doesn't make sense. Not to me.'

'Archdeacon, I wonder if you'd like to comment,' said Mrs. Fitzpatrick, turning hesitantly to Dorothy Proud. The Archdeacon smiled amiably and joined the platform party around the lectern.

'Good evening everyone,' she began, 'I welcome the opportunity to explain the Church Academy proposal to you all.' A collective sigh escaped the parents listening to her.

'In recent years,' she continued, 'Our energies in the Diocese have been very much taken up by the buildings. As you know, the Church has very limited resources and St Michael's has proved a very challenging project. Three schools came together at the time of re-organisation but unfortunately the new premises were not completed until last year.'

Dennis Matthews interrupted.

'I'm sorry, Archdeacon, we've heard all this before. What you've got to realise is that not one person here wants this academy. You don't have a single supporter. What we want is an LA with the guts to get behind the parents.'

Loud applause greeted his words.

'I'm very sorry but you must face facts, however disagreeable. You cannot carry on as you are. The DCSF has made it very clear – there will be an academy on this site by September 2009.'

There was uproar, with shouted comments and jeers. Parents talked amongst themselves, ignoring Mrs. Fitzpatrick's pleas for silence. When the noise eventually subsided, Helen Lightfoot spoke up.

'You've not answered my question. Why on earth did you appoint Mrs. Sparkler?'

'We can't discuss individual people here,' said Mrs. Fitzpatrick firmly.

'I have to tell you the answer is very straightforward,' said the Archdeacon, unabashed by the noisy reaction that accompanied her words. 'As sponsors, we are obliged to get you the very best headteacher that can be found.'

'She's not a Christian,' shouted a voice.

'She was sacked from her last job,' shouted someone else.

Paul Slater took a firm step forward.

'Look, this really is most important. We're here to gather information on the closure issue, not to debate the merits of the academy,' he said. 'This is a consultation on whether the school should close.'

An elderly man in a tweed coat raised his hand.

'I'm Fred Davies,' he said. 'I've been a member of the governing body here since St. Michael's started. We don't have faith in this consultation because we've been treated so badly. The Diocese has done a cloak and dagger job here, we don't trust them. Is there any real chance that you'll change you mind?'

'Oh yes. There is a definite option for not closing if there is not enough stakeholder support for the proposal,' answered the Director. 'In my report, I'll fully reflect the representations that have been made in this part of the process. I'll give a fair and balanced report on your points. And cabinet members may decide to look for other proposals.'

'On another point,' said the governor, 'How long do you think it takes to turn a school round?'

'Around three years,' answered the Director, 'though that's only rule of thumb.'

'So how is Isobel Allen supposed to do the job in three or four months? In fairness, she should be given the same time as anyone else,' said Fred Davies.

Paul Slater shook his head. A mother rose reluctantly to her feet.

'I'm Debbie Smith, and my son Damian started here in September. We chose St. Michael's very carefully. We visited other schools but this one got our vote. Mrs. Allen explained the changes she was going to make and we were very impressed. She's kept all her promises. Damian's very happy. We're very pleased with how he's getting on. You've spent the whole evening rubbishing the school and want to start again from scratch. I don't think you should have the right.'

When she finished speaking there was silence.

'There's one more thing,' said a man near the front, 'I don't think organisations cope that well with all this change. What happens to football clubs that have three managers in a year? They get relegated. What happens to businesses that have three CEOs in a year? They go broke. What are Mrs. Sparkler's chances after all this?'

'Well, thank you,' began Mrs. Fitzpatrick, after a pause. 'We've more or less used up our time and you've been very clear about your feelings in this matter.'

'Can I speak?' asked a sixth former who had listened quietly throughout the meeting. 'You've heard from everyone except the students. We've not been consulted by anyone. No one's asked us. But we don't want St. Michael's to change. Mrs. Allen's a great head and she's made a big difference in a short time. If this academy goes ahead everyone will be demoralised, the teachers will give up and all the good work will be wasted. We don't want that to happen. We like it the way it is.'

'You've not asked the Asians either,' shouted a voice, 'There's not one brown face here.'

'Only half the community missing then,' said someone else as people began to put on their coats and make for the exits.

The Problems of Reform

St. Michael's has hovered on the edge of Ofsted purgatory since the re-organisation that created it and continues to struggle with a variety of disadvantages. For example, the school is urban and serves wards that are amongst the 15 per cent most deprived in England. Since its formation, St. Michael's has been placed at the bottom of the local hierarchy of schools and is associated in the public mind with low status housing and poor academic performance. As a result, St. Michael's has failed over time to recruit a fair share of able students from aspirational families and is not perceived as an attractive destination for teachers starting their careers or seeking promotion. Temporary and agency staff have covered many vacancies, especially in science and languages. The Thornton reorganisation, completed five years ago, merged middle and upper schools across the town into larger and more complex establishments, with many teachers lacking experience of GCSE and A Level examinations. A phased building programme was mismanaged, so that schools like St Michael's experienced rapid growth within temporary or incomplete accommodation. Despite these difficulties, St. Michael's has not suffered from falling rolls. School accommodation in Thornton is tightly managed, so there is a close fit between the available number of places and demand.

The multiple, interacting problems detailed above explain, however, why government agencies have achieved so little, so far, at St. Michael's, despite their extensive powers and a longstanding commitment to deal with failing schools and unsatisfactory conditions for learning. Despite many initiatives, endemic sources of failure undermine hopes of sustained academic success. School hierarchies reflect long-term social and economic trends and reinforce the differentiation produced by local housing markets. As a result, the intake of schools at the bottom of the league is typically biased towards those children who have the least chance of success and the least to gain by participating in competitive tests and examinations. This discourages teachers and contributes to the formation of a culture of low expectations based on what seems like hard reality to those involved. In these circumstances, school leaders and teachers are likely to lack the capability to adopt effective strategies, whatever their source.

The implementation of government intervention may also contribute to the failure of reform. Policy requires, for example, that government agencies act as if these social influences on learning do not exist. Policy-makers believe poverty is an incidental variable, unlikely to have a significant impact on effective schools and teachers. The result is that many policies are unrealistic and exacerbate the problems they are intended to solve. Parental choice is encouraged, therefore, although the effect is to increase the differentiation between school intakes and to concentrate poverty in unmanageable pockets at the bottom of the performance tables. In reality, however, there is little choice for the less discerning family, because the number of school places is strictly regulated on grounds of economy. Children born into poor families tend to end up trapped in their own estates and schools.

The denial of poverty as a key determinant of educational responses and outcomes has a similar impact on policies designed to improve the conditions for learning. The Ofsted Framework provides a standardised template that is applied across the country, as if the children at St. Michael's are the same as those in leafy, southern suburbia and as if the same curriculum and methods are effective for the full ability range.

The story of St. Michael's also highlights the remarkable number of different agencies and partners involved in school reform and shows how these do not always communicate effectively with one another and are sometimes less than well coordinated. Responsibility for intervention in this case is divided between the DCSF, Ofsted, the LA and the Diocese. The LA mismanaged the Thornton reorganisation. The Diocese did not deal quickly or effectively with the old head, misled Isobel Allen into believing that she was trusted to deal with the school's problems and would have time to turn the school around, and failed to consult the parents before adopting the academy proposal. Ofsted issued a Notice to Improve in 2005, but there was a long delay before the school was placed in Special Measures in 2008. In this case, Ofsted has spread discomfort and unease over a period of years, contributing very little of positive value.

The DCSF decided to forge ahead with a Church Academy proposal, completely disregarding what was happening in the school. The parents' views and wishes were discounted in advance. As the record of the consultation meeting shows, however, the parents were articulate in opposing the closure of their school, and engaged in local democratic debate with rare passion and commitment. Governments are unwise to ignore such widely held and well-argued opinions. In a case like this, public service reform has contributed to a climate where people withdraw from the democratic process in disgust. With their views ignored, parents are unlikely to work with the head appointed to an academy they opposed from the beginning. Reformers like Adonis (2008) have emphasised the value of markets and parental choice in bringing about improvement, but have been inclined to disregard local voices when implementing reorganisations, closures and new buildings.

The human cost of educational reorganisations is not well understood by those instigating them but casualties experience at first hand what it means to be interviewed to see whether you are suitable to continue working, to be transplanted forcibly from one environment to another, or to lose your job, or to suffer mental and physical illness. The authorities regard these consequences as a necessary step in the road to school improvement but the benefits of a wholesale purge are sometimes less than obvious, while the disruptive impact on teachers and children may continue for years. Thornton's reorganisation four years ago created major management challenges for the enlarged establishments and caused many teachers to leave the profession. Special measures status often leads to a purge of teachers but the benefits can be short-lived if a school's fundamental challenges are unchanged. Calderdale Council, for example, took the decision to close The Ridings School in Halifax in 2007 after more than ten years that included special measures and numerous other initiatives to raise achievement.

At St. Michael's, Isobel Allen was close to being discarded within three months of taking up her post, not because she was failing or had committed some impropriety, but because the Diocese did not explain what was going on and because the government agenda demands the creation of academies. As a result, a successful and experienced headteacher has been damaged for no good reason and her work to improve St. Michael's might be thrown away. This is a remarkable development, given the acute shortage of school leaders prepared to work in challenging circumstances. Soon her colleagues will experience a similar shock as they apply for vacancies in their own school for the second time in four years. St. Michael's provides a good example of clumsy and incompetent reforms that have been more damaging than the issues they were designed to correct.

The Church Academy sponsors were unable to answer Martha Rainthorpe when she claimed that St. Michael's already enjoyed 'strong leadership', the most tangible of the advantages believed to be associated with academies. Other parents asked about the risk of an abrupt and unwelcome change of direction, especially as the new head's less than impressive reputation has travelled ahead of her, but no satisfactory reply was given. Academies may have a better than average chance of securing 'strong leadership' but their recruitment success seems to depend on inflating salaries to attract candidates who may otherwise have performed equally well elsewhere. Academies inflate costs but their benefits remain mysteriously intangible.

Although the academy programme has been driven forward with determination and speed, there is no real evidence that it represents a distinctive or proven solution to the problems of reform. As PricewaterhouseCoopers point out:

> Academies themselves represent a diverse group of institutions; they are borne out of diverse circumstances, have different specialisms and cultures, and are led and governed in different ways, based on different models. (PwC, 2006:ii)

Ministers believe academies will solve the troubles found in challenging locations but so far have been unable to explain why new governance arrangements and new buildings in themselves should improve the conditions that matter for learning. The imbroglio at St. Michael's provides a warning that Academy governance may prove no more satisfactory than other models when stakeholders and the community disagree. The Church Academy sponsors at St. Michael's include partners implicated in the school's previous mismanagement. In the eyes of many local parents, these sponsors are also contaminated by their partisanship in promoting an unwanted and unloved academy in Thornton. Why should the Diocese and LA do better second time round?

This case study suggests, therefore, that a number of related factors are compromising the success of school reform initiatives at local level, especially those intended to improve education in disadvantaged and challenging circumstances. The most significant of these are:

■ *Fragmentation within the reform apparatus*
Operationally independent agencies have overlapping roles and responsibilities that frustrate attempts at coordination. New policy initiatives lead to confused and contradictory priorities.

■ *Assumptions about effectiveness and improvement*
Despite frequent Ministerial assertions to the contrary, poverty remains an unevenly distributed and important influence on learning. In consequence, standardised recommendations based on effectiveness research do not yield the expected outcomes, especially in terms of test and examination results.

■ *Assumptions about choice and markets*
A tenet of school reform is that the competition between institutions in a free market improves quality, choice and client outcomes. In reality, surplus places are removed to ensure that school accommodation is provided on a cost efficient basis. This undermines market choice because parents often find it impossible to secure places in popular schools or even in schools outside their own neighbourhoods. As a result, social geography has become an ever more important influence on education.

■ *Aims and purposes of policy initiatives*
The Academy programme is an example of a policy that lacks a closely specified educational rationale. Research has failed to confirm convincing links between the various features associated with academy organisation and improved student outcomes. There is little evidence that increased competition between schools has a beneficial impact on learning and teaching. The driving force behind the programme seems to be the supposed financial benefits associated with sponsorship.

■ *Defining success and failure*
Despite the government's assumption that there is an optimal state of effectiveness, towards which all schools may aspire, the chosen measures of that effectiveness regularly change. There is a ceaseless game in which performance thresholds are altered as soon as schools work out how to achieve them. The GCSE 5 A*-C grades

benchmark must now include English and Mathematics. The 2008 criteria for entry to the High Performing Specialist Schools programme include revised attainment thresholds that increase the risk of losing funds if the results do not improve (PwC, 2008).

Ofsted inspection schedules are frequently adjusted (most recently in 2009) to ensure sustained pressure rather than timeless fair judgement. Ofsted claims that the latest framework 'raises the bar because it raises expectations' and insists that no excuses will be accepted for underachievement (Dennis, 2009:16). All the once objective measures of effectiveness have been mobilised to drive the system towards ever-improving test and examination performance. As a result, 'failure' has become an inescapable, permanent feature of the system, with schools judged in terms of their ability to adapt to ever more demanding targets.

Is the school the problem?

Although overall school performance has been the main focus of government attention, the 2002 results from the OECD's Programme for International Student Assessment (PISA) show that as much as 80 per cent of the variation in achievement among UK students appears within rather than between schools. In-school variance was four times greater than that occurring between schools (TDA, 2009).

It seems that until very recently attempts to improve examination results have been chasing the wrong target and that 'failure' is a more complex phenomenon than reformers have allowed.

School reform has thus become circular and self-defeating. Each advance highlights those who have not advanced enough, so that the illusion of perpetual success generates the reality of endless failure, the very opposite of Sir Michael Barber's ambition in 1995. This is not a helpful climate for school and classroom improvement, nor for children trapped in a fiercely competitive and market driven education system.

5

Bastards and Prophets

Leadership and Modernisation

A passionate belief in leadership and modernisation has been fundamental to the New Labour project, and to the NPM approach that has unfolded since 1997. New public managers are expected to emulate private sector entrepreneurs, and to transform 'top-heavy and ossified structures' into 'flexible entities driven by values, missions, visions and charismatic personal example' (Clarke and Newman, 1997:36). Born-again leaders and managers are supposed to be missionaries, committed to use their delegated power to transform the culture, organisation and performance of their service units.

This chapter explores the role of 'leadership' in school reform, and draws on four individual school case studies to review how these expectations have worked out in reality; and in the light of the evidence asks whether leadership can escape or transcend the chaos induced by over-ambitious government agencies and misconceived bureaucratic initiatives. Are heads empowered as prophets of a new social order, as the rhetoric of school reform asserts, or have they become 'bastard leaders', conduits of government policy asked to manage output and performance rather than direct 'the moral and value basis' of children's education (Wright, 2001:278)?

The government assumes that when school heads, council managers and hospital administrators become 'social entrepreneurs', eager to define and solve social problems in their communities, many transformational benefits will follow. Leadership, and the transformation invariably associated with it in government rhetoric, have become, therefore, dominant themes in the political discourse of public sector reform. New leaders and managers are expected to act as catalysts, releasing human potential and transforming the quality and competitiveness of their organisations (Peters and Waterman, 1995). From the Prime Minister downwards, there has been an expectation that school leaders should create visions of transformed communities, distribute leadership and raise their followers to new levels of commitment and achievement (Blair, 2001; Miliband, 2002). Friendly academics have encouraged government agencies in their confident belief that heads can transform the context, organisation and results of their schools, so that cruising, strolling, and struggling schools are turned round and previously elusive effectiveness characteristics are firmly embedded (Stoll and Fink, 1995; Fullan, 2003).

In 1996, the Teacher Training Agency (TTA) commissioned the consultancy company Hay McBer to research and develop appropriate leadership models for UK schools and colleges, as the foundation for a new training initiative, the Leadership Programme for Serving Heads (LPSH). The resulting Hay models and training, with their emphasis on headteacher personality characteristics, leadership styles and school climate, were transferred to the NCSL in 2001 and have permeated the college's menu ever since, including the latest version of LPSH, Head for the Future. The NCSL (2001, 2003a) recommends that individual leaders, or groups of leaders empowered by their heads, select styles to induce heightened motivation and change, especially in student examination outcomes. Less successful heads are encouraged to learn from high performers and to seamlessly apply the lessons to their own schools.

Although Hay completed interviews with heads and stakeholders and made a serious attempt to locate their models in UK school leadership, the main sources for LPSH were research into human motivation conducted at Harvard in the 1960s, and commercial training programmes that had been available on the international market for some years (Litwin and Stringer, 1968; Barker, 2005). Hay developed a programme very similar to LPSH for the State of Victoria in Australia, and used the early results as evidence of success when negotiating with the British authorities. Consultancy firms work with a wide variety of companies in a range of contexts, so there is an inevitable tendency for their training and development activities to stress transferable skills that are equally appropriate for any industry or business environment.

Consultants like Hay McBer draw heavily, therefore, on psychological research to inform management programmes that are equally valid, or at least plausible, in any workplace. LPSH comes complete with a suite of questionnaires, 360° feedback, diagnostic data, and a set of charts that display participants' leadership styles and their positive or negative impact on motivation, as measured by the organisational climate. This is the familiar world of personnel management, where batteries of psychological and intelligence tests provide an apparently scientific basis for employee selection and development. Statistical techniques are applied to the raw data derived from the LPSH questionnaires, and impart an apparent measure of objectivity to the results and validate programme claims. Provided they adopt the appropriate combination of styles in the various situations they encounter, leaders are believed to arouse and mobilise positive motivation that improves performance.

This psychological approach was especially attractive for the British government as it prepared to reform the public sector. Here was a scientific, transferable methodology, used by hugely profitable corporations in the US to equip the great leaders who turned round failing rust-belt and smokestack industries in the 1980s and 1990s (Peters, 1989). Their success was tangible evidence of a cultural revolution that could be achieved in schools, hospitals and council offices. Business schools and consultants are consistent and clear in their message that management skills can be improved and used to transform the public sector mindset that seems a major obstacle to high quality services. Mabey and Ramirez (2004:9), for example, claim to have found 'strong statistical evidence that management development leads to superior organisational performance across companies of all sizes, sectors and national location'.

Leadership and Motivation

Litwin and Stringer's (1968) research at Harvard Business School uncovered an essential psychological mechanism believed to explain how leaders influence followers. The motivational profiles of workers in three simulated companies were measured before and after an eight-day business game. Each company director adopted a distinctive combination of styles. The investigators discovered that although individuals had different motivational profiles before the experiment began, the workers in each company responded in similar ways to their director's leadership behaviour during the game (Barker, 2005).

One director adopted coercive and pacesetting styles. His attempts at close control and regulation proved counter-productive and aroused his employees' power motivation in ways that led to a strike and the premature end of the experiment. The second director set out to be a 'people person' and used democratic and affiliative styles to promote friendly relationships and team spirit. Employees treated work as a party and gave achievement and standards a low priority. The third director emphasised vision and direction (the authoritative style) and coached workers so they dedicated themselves to high standards and performance. His company was easily the most successful. The experiment led Litwin and Stringer to believe that leadership styles have stable, consistent and predictable effects on what they called the 'climate' for employees, strongly influencing their ability to perform well. Workplace climates are established surprisingly quickly and seem to have marked effects on motivation, performance and job satisfaction (Litwin and Stringer, 1968).

The NCSL (2003b:10-12) has defined these styles and climate dimensions in plain language so that leaders can understand and calculate their impact on others. The prized authoritative style, for example, is described as 'providing long-term direction and vision for staff' and leaders demonstrating the style use direction more than directives. When using this style, a leader invites staff to contribute their ideas but persuades them to share the vision by explaining how chosen courses of action are in the school's long-term best interests. S/he monitors progress towards desired goals and provides balanced feedback to sustain and increase motivation (NCSL, 2003a, Day 1, p61).

The style has a generally positive impact, improving, for example, flexibility (no unnecessary procedures and practices; new ideas encouraged) and responsibility (no need to check everything with the boss; scope to take calculated risks). The NCSL concludes that excellent leaders adopt styles that improve the climate, arouse the achievement motive (meeting or exceeding a standard of excellence and/or improving one's performance) and produce high performing schools and colleges (NCSL, 2003a, 2003b).

Transformational and Distributed Leadership

The Hay/NCSL models are thus consistent with Bass's theory of transformational leadership. Leaders who adopt predominantly authoritative and coaching styles are said to produce strongly positive workplace climates, and so achieve the four types of influence associated with transformation. Leaders should provide role models for their colleagues through *idealised influence*. They should use *inspirational motivation* to arouse team spirit and to increase commitment to organisational goals and vision. Leaders should also stimulate followers intellectually so they question assumptions and reframe problems. They should give *individualised consideration* to followers through appropriate coaching and mentoring (Bass and Avolio, eds, 1994:2-4).

Academics who see authoritative school leadership as a major source of change and improved performance are explicit about the typical actions associated with transformational models. Leaders should mobilise commitment to an explicit vision, coach staff to increase their leadership capacity, and encourage participatory decision-making (Gold *et al*, 2003). As in Bass's transformational theory, leaders are supposed to offer intellectual stimulation and individualised support as they develop the organisation, and should strengthen the school's collaborative culture. They should also provide instructional guidance while empowering others to make significant decisions. Successful leaders 'don't impose goals but work with others to create a shared sense of purpose and direction', and galvanise 'effort around ambitious goals ... by establishing conditions that support teachers.' Leaders' organisational impact is mediated through middle leaders, teachers, and the internal conditions they develop (Leithwood and Riehl, 2003:2-3).

As time has gone on, however, earlier conceptions of transformational leadership have had to be extended or revised, because 'there is no evidence to suggest that, on its own, it brings about anything but modest improved consequences for pupil outcomes'. Leaders are encouraged, therefore, to give particular attention to instructional issues, and to concentrate on the 'behaviours of staff as they engage in activities directly affecting the quality of teaching and learning' (Gold *et al*, 2003: 129).

In recent years, the NCSL has promoted distributed leadership, believing that all professionals are potential leaders, able to contribute to organisational change and improvement. The distributed model presents leadership as the 'emergent property of a group or network of interacting individuals' rather than as the work of a single heroic or charismatic figure. When colleagues contribute their initiative and expertise, the outcome should be greater than the sum of their individual actions. Valuable expertise is 'distributed across the many, not the few' and should be mobilised to support the common cause of improved effectiveness (Bennett *et al*, 2003:7).

Further studies have added to this persuasive picture of inspirational leaders working at all levels to transform their schools. A National Foundation for Educational Research (NFER) evaluation of 20 high-performing specialist schools found that, rather than implementing a shopping list of improvements, successful multi-skilled heads were encouraging a greater 'interconnectedness'. Multiple inputs were integrated into a wider vision so that 'superb student – teacher relations', 'a shared sense of vision', and 'genuine working together' generated an institutional buzz. Energetic, visionary leadership, a focus on the individual student, the active use of performance data, a broad and flexible curriculum, and enhanced status and resources contributed to a climate where teachers were prepared to go 'the extra mile' (Judkins and Rudd, 2005:4).

An NCSL-sponsored enquiry into learning-centred leadership confirmed the central role of the headteacher and leadership team, illustrated the extent to which school culture facilitates school improvement, and indicated the need to concentrate on raising achievement (Madison and Allison, 2004). Another study found that in all types of schools the effective use of data was valuable in challenging the expectations of staff and children and in stimulating questions and discussion that prompt improvement (Kirkup *et al*, 2005).

The government, its agencies and sympathetic academics have established, therefore, a consistent set of recommendations about school leaders and leadership, and cultivate the impression that we know a great deal about how to improve and transform educational organisations. Leithwood and Riehl (2003) describe with confidence 'What We Know About Successful School Leadership'; Hopkins (2007) writes as if we were in possession of a secret formula that can be applied to make 'Every School a Great School'. The official position is that we know how to improve motivation and overcome poor performance. Provided school leaders learn from the example of high performing heads and adopt the right combination of styles, we can expect the examination results to go up year on year.

Critical Perspectives

These claims are open to a number of criticisms. The Hay/NCSL models purport to be scientific, but no experiment has been conducted in UK schools to confirm or refute the proposition that certain types of leadership can transform motivation and performance. Evaluations have been concerned with the quality of programmes, not their effectiveness in 'raising standards'. This may be because Hay Group's intellectual property rights have precluded a rigorous evaluation of NCSL impact. There is the additional concern that despite the ready availability of performance data, the NCSL has failed to gather basic information about trends at schools providing LPSH participants. Instead, investigators have relied on repeated observations to confirm their prediction (i.e that leadership improves effectiveness), rejecting Karl Popper's argument that theory cannot be 'inferred from empirical evidence' (1963:54). In his opinion, the true function of observations and experiments in science is to test our hypotheses, not to confirm what we think we know.

There is the further problem that despite their surface similarity, the various transformational models have not been constructed in ways that are easily tested, confirmed or refuted. Leaders are believed to influence followers through psychological mechanisms that we are beginning to understand, but the concept of transformation is ambiguous and has become ever more slippery as leadership has evolved through its heroic, charismatic and distributed incarnations. The nature of the desired transformation has not been defined and no agency has attempted to estimate the extra effectiveness expected to result from better leadership (Dunford, 2002). It is unclear how improvements in climate and motivation are translated into enhanced teaching and increases in test and examination results.

Critics also complain that the language of transformation disguises the exploitative potential of techniques that produce heightened motivation, intense commitment and the submergence of the self in corporate objectives (Ball, 2003b). Allix believes that transformational leadership is just as instrumental and manipulative as transactional leadership because the leader's aims and needs are privileged over others' subjective wishes. The transformational leader, he believes, employs an emotionally charged version of transactional leadership to achieve domination (2000:15-18). Morrison states this more bluntly; he believes that transactional and transformational approaches are both 'variants of a teleological determinism, and command and control mentalities' (2002:69).

The working assumption of the transformational vision is that all our problems can be solved through the harmonious alignment of people and organisations in the pursuit of prescribed policy goals. Critics believe, however, that conflict is an inevitable feature of social organisations, and that schools are limited in their ability to deliver the goals and targets that are set for them. Teachers have varied personal and professional values and interests and also belong to organisations that are loose-coupled. The result is a 'feasibility gap between centrally determined policies and the possibility of their faithful implementation' (Hoyle, 1986; Weick, 1988; Hoyle and Wallace, 2007:11).

Transforming Schools

Despite these reservations and concerns, it is not hard to find examples of school leaders who are said to have transformed their schools by means similar to those described and explained by the Hay/NCSL models. The heads' reported behaviour in these examples is also consistent with other accounts of transformational and distributed leadership. By adopting authoritative and coaching styles, a number of excellent heads seem to have brought about important and profound changes with remarkable speed, leading previously struggling institutions to newfound respectability and success.

The case studies (detailed in Table 2[11] overleaf) examine the role of six individual head teachers who worked to transform their schools. To what extent did the leadership action observed by stakeholders match NCSL models? Were the schools transformed? Did test and examination results improve as official models predict?

The data presented relates to four schools:

- *Hillside*: A small 11-16 school in a disadvantaged urban area. Long-term decline and poor leadership resulted in Special Measures. Two new heads worked to transform Hillside over a three-year period.

- *Norcross*: A struggling 11-18 comprehensive in a former coal-field. One head battled for sixteen years to implement government recommendations and improve examination results.

- *Felix Holt*: A small 11-18 ex-secondary modern school in a southern county. Over a seventeen-year period, Felix Holt was transformed, attracting more able students and more than doubling in size.

- *The Shire*: A small 11-18 rural comprehensive in the south. With exceptional leadership, The Shire grew, established itself in Ofsted terms as an 'outstanding school', and attracted students from a wide area.

School Circumstances

Although Hillside and Norcross belong to disadvantaged urban land-scapes, they are located on extensive, windy playing fields near arterial roads leading out of town. Beneath the suburban surface, however, both serve council estates blighted by post-industrial poverty as well as pockets of owner occupation. Ofsted described the Norcross hamlet as 'very socially deprived', with the recent closure of the local coalmine contributing to worsening employment opportunities.

At the time of the study, Hillside was placed in special measures be-cause 'weaknesses arise from serious shortcomings in the quality of leadership and management' (Ofsted Report), while the LA decided the school should close as part of a plan to reduce the number of surplus places in the district. A Parents' Action Group (PAG) was established to fight the closure and two new, acting heads (Mr. Goodlad for a term;

Table 2: Case Study Schools

School Case Study / *Year of Publication:*	Hillside *(2003, 2005)*	Norcross *(2009a)*	Felix Holt *(2006)*	The Shire *(2007)*
Location/type	*11-16 co-educational comprehensive (Midlands)*	*11-18 co-educational comprehensive; later specialist college (North)*	*11-18 co-educational *GM comprehensive; later specialist college (South East)*	*11-18 co-educational *GM comprehensive; later specialist college (South West)*
Period covered by the study	*5 years*	*16 years*	*17 years*	*11 years*
Ofsted status at start	*Special measures*	*None*	*None*	*None*
Ofsted status at end	*None*	*None*	*None*	*Listed as 'outstanding'*
Size at start	*490*	*850*	*495*	*594*
Size at end	*560*	*1450*	*1109*	*925*
% 5A*-C grades cf national average: start and finish	*-17.5%* *-16.9%*	*-21%* *-17%*	*-22%* *+3%*	*+2%* *+9%*
Average FSM entitlement	*16%*	*27%*	*10%*	*11%*
Pseudonym of Head(s)	*Mr. Goodlad (1 term)* *Mr. Moore (2 years)*	*Mr. Turner (17 years)*	*H2 (6 years in post)* *H3 (10 years in post)*	*Ms Thomson (11 years)*

*GM: Grant Maintained

then Mr. Moore for two years) led an eventually successful campaign to rescue Hillside from special measures and avoid closure.

When Mr. Turner was appointed, Norcross was struggling. About 30 children a year migrated from seven local primaries to more popular local schools. Mr. Turner said that the primary schools themselves were exceptionally poor and contributed to underachievement in the area. Governors had little confidence in the previous head or the teachers, not least because of the very poor examination results (8.2% achieved 5A*-C grades in 1989).

During the early 1990s, Felix Holt and The Shire were small and declining, with low morale and disappointing GCSE results. Located in county authorities, they served relatively prosperous, mobile communities but able pupils and their families were inclined to choose other, more prestigious destinations. At Felix Holt, the intake shrank from 180 in 1985 to less than 100 by 1992. According to a long-serving teacher, the school suffered from a persistent 'secondary modern image' and all the primaries were 'steering low ability to us ... able siblings were sent to other places'. The governors feared the school was on the county's 'chop list'.

The long serving, retiring heads of these schools showed similar signs of 'disenchantment', resulting in colleagues noticing their loss of motivation, deteriorating health, including symptoms of stress, and resistance to change (Day and Bakioğlu, 1996). Teachers commented on the heads' coercive styles and the lack of consultation. The old head at Hillside, for example, 'could be rude, blunt, aggressive' and his 'method was too strict and it made the school feel gloomy and not really enthusiastic'. The staff did not like to contribute at meetings because the head would tell them off in public. At Felix Holt the head 'never left his office'. Parents and teachers commented on his 'poor speeches at parents' evenings' and believed he was presiding over the school's slide to the 'bottom of the local pecking order'. The poor morale, motivation and climate reported seem consistent with expectations from the Hay/ NCSL models.

Leadership Characteristics, Styles and Climates

All six new heads adopted positive styles and were praised in glowing terms by the governors, parents, teachers and students interviewed. Ms.

Thomson made an immediate impression at The Shire and aroused strong loyalty in her colleagues:

> (She) is a remarkable person ... she's so wonderful at the decisions, talking to people, knowing what is the best way to go, how to approach the staff – I've worked for a lot of people, she's so focused, a wonderful person to work for – makes the right decisions at the right times – the leadership pulls everyone together.

At Felix Holt the new head (H2) was seen as a 'new broom sweeping clean, very young, all guns blazing, very enthusiastic' and possessing 'boundless energy to get things done'. He was 'like Lenny Henry turning round a failing school ... he was a good communicator' and had 'fantastic leadership skills'. He was 'incredibly charismatic, you wanted to work for him, he was dynamic and wanted the school to go places'. Norcross teachers described Mr. Turner as intensely 'hands on' and cited his passion, energy and commitment as particular strengths. He was highly visible around the school and was frequently found in classrooms and corridors or out supervising at break and lunchtime.

Although he was acting head for just one term at Hillside, Mr. Goodlad was also very active and highly visible. He introduced a daily briefing to inform and involve the staff, and started a student council to work on a new behaviour code. Parents remembered him as 'a very loveable man ... incredibly open, excitable, boyish, lots of humour, loads of energy and *joie de vivre*'. His successor, Mr. Moore, concentrated on implementing the Ofsted action plan, rather than emulating Mr. Goodlad's high impact style, but teachers later remembered that

> ...we have been in on everything and he has involved us in everything and he has actually asked our opinions and consulted us on things which has felt nice because it seems like he respects us as individuals.

When H3 succeeded H2 at Felix Holt in 1993, he was not received as an adequate replacement. H3 was nothing like as 'upfront, out and about' as the previous head. But he was determined and he eventually replaced the old senior management team that had resisted his changes. His new team concentrated initially on the classroom and revised the teaching and learning reviews. Staff said they now had much greater input and were helped to set their own targets. A special needs teacher noted that 'it's a very different school, there's been a great increase in teacher expectations'. An assistant head reflected that H3 'gives you the ammunition, allows you to take the glory' so that colleagues 'want to work hard' because 'you're encouraged, it builds up your belief'.

Coaching styles were also evident. At Hillside, one teacher remembered that Mr. Moore coached the staff so they understood what Ofsted inspectors were looking for and helped prepare them for monitoring visits. Another noted that:

> We had been taught the command style of teaching by the old head but Mr. Moore is about 'get a partner, discuss, talk about, see what things you can come up with'. He is very up to date on things that are going on.

At The Shire, the head emphasised developing people, admitting that 'from the moment I meet people I'm assessing them for development and what they can do in the future'. An assistant head said he felt 'valued and I've been given the confidence, the training and the belief to do what's needed'.

Five of the six heads included in the case studies had, therefore, an immediate, strongly positive impact on motivation, adopting authoritative and coaching styles and offering a clearly defined vision for progress. They quickly earned the respect of their school communities. At Felix Holt, however, H3 took longer to establish himself. He was frustrated by resistance from teachers who were closely associated with the previous regime and devoted considerable attention to internal politics. Once his own team was in place, however, H3 was able to communicate his vision and motivate his colleagues through his strong emphasis on classroom learning. The children at Felix Holt 'see the school as high achieving and valued; they are told it so often that they perform to expectations'.

The positive climate effects reported in these studies were sustained over time, though changes of personnel were sometimes important in removing resistance. At Felix Holt, as we have seen, and also at Norcross, there are clear examples of deputies and other senior colleagues who behaved in ways that damaged the trust needed for successful distributed leadership. Mr. Turner had skirted round his Norcross deputies for eight years before realising they were compromising the otherwise positive features of the school. One deputy head was described as lazy but amiable, the other was seen as 'nasty for the sake of being nasty'. With the help of a consultant, Mr. Turner removed both men, in the process creating a changed culture where 'teachers no longer expect the leadership team to be lazy and have no impact'.

Ms. Thomson was more fortunate. From the beginning, leadership was dispersed widely across the school and 'huge responsibility' was distributed to the staff. The leadership team at The Shire were said to trust the middle managers and a classroom teacher has 'the feeling she (the head) trusts in the teachers' judgement and independence, though we work as a team'. A newly qualified teacher noticed that 'we are there as a group ... I never get the feeling that I'm being ordered or told'.

During the research for the case studies, Mr. Moore, Mr. Turner and Ms. Thomson provided access to their LPSH diagnostic data. This confirmed their predominant use of authoritative and coaching styles, and gave a clear indication of the exceptionally positive climates created in their schools.

School Outcomes

The leadership actions reported in these case studies are similar, therefore, to the behaviour researchers have observed at other successful schools, and matches expectations based on the Hay/NCSL models. The heads selected a mix of predominantly authoritative and coaching styles to create a positive climate that improved motivation and engagement. They forged a 'shared sense of purpose and direction' and worked to create conditions that support teachers. Leadership was distributed so that everyone felt involved and the expertise of 'the many, not the few' was mobilised. In each case, teachers, students and parents expressed a strong sense of a 'genuine working together' and a willingness to go 'the extra mile' (Gold *et al*, 2003; Leithwood and Riehl, 2003; Judkins and Rudd, 2005).

All those interviewed agreed that this consistent, positive leadership approach brought about great improvements in the case study schools. Successive Ofsted inspections confirmed the views of participants. Ofsted found The Shire to be 'very good and extremely effective' with 'many outstanding features'. Clear vision and strong leadership were said to have a major impact on improving standards of attainment. Norcross was praised for steady improvements in teaching and learning and Mr. Turner's strong and effective leadership was regularly commended. At Felix Holt:

> The headteacher (H3) shares his passion for learning with the senior leadership team and faculty leaders. He sets a very clear direction for improvement and his demanding approach to delegated management has successfully challenged leaders to raise standards and achievement, and secured good personal development across the school.

Ofsted monitored Hillside closely through its period in special measures. HMI reported that the school's effectiveness was transformed. The senior management team provided strong leadership and direction; the quality of teaching was sound or better in nine out of ten lessons and good in 40 per cent; behaviour was also good.

At all the schools there was also more tangible evidence of improvement. The number on roll increased very substantially at Norcross (by 600), Felix Holt (by 614) and The Shire (by 331). According to one teacher at The Shire, the school has become 'bigger, more popular, the results are very good ... surrounding villages hear about it and that's when you pull in the more middle class people'. Norcross and Felix Holt became oversubscribed, and also recruited a higher proportion of children from aspiring homes. The sixth form at The Shire increased from 71 in 1994 to 164 in 2005; at Norcross the post-sixteen enrolment rose from 59 in 1990 to 250 in 2006; and at Felix Holt the post-sixteen numbers almost trebled over a 12 year period. At Hillside the number on roll increased by 14 per cent in three years. In all four cases, these improved numbers were the result of competitive success and the schools' improved ranking within their neighbourhoods.

All four heads also engineered changes of status for their schools and secured important funding to ensure improvements in buildings and facilities. At Hillside, Mr. Goodlad built a smart reception area and invested in a new computer suite, while Mr. Moore led the school out of special measures and persuaded the LA to expand the school rather than close it. Under Mr. Turner's leadership, Norcross became a specialist performing arts college and accommodated the town's City Learning Centre. H2 secured GMS status at Felix Holt and in partnership with the local council embarked on an ambitious community leisure project. H3 rescued the scheme when financial disaster seemed likely, and also bid successfully for specialist science college status. He then persuaded the LA to fund an impressive new science block. At The Shire, the premises and facilities were greatly improved. Specialist language college recognition has helped the school to change its status and become an important centre for the local rural community.

Participants and stakeholders were also keen to praise the improved quality of teaching and learning at these schools, and their views were invariably confirmed by relevant Ofsted inspection reports. Students commented frequently on the 'amazing changes' and improvements that 'are happening all the time'. At Hillside, HMI found the teaching 'impressive overall'; at Norcross, the teachers' commitment was described as 'high, fantastic'; at Felix Holt, inspectors reported that 'students achieve well due to good teaching and their positive attitudes and behaviour'; at The Shire, the students' behaviour was found to be 'outstanding', while teaching and learning were 'good or better in 80 per cent of the 172 lessons seen ... no lessons were less than satisfactory.' One student commented that his teachers were so good that he felt sorry for 'my friends who tell me about other schools'.

Student Outcomes

Close scrutiny of the available performance data reveals, however, that despite these strong qualitative improvements, especially in teaching and learning, none of the four schools managed to achieve a higher level of effectiveness in terms of student test and examination outcomes. Like the 12 case study schools investigated by Gray *et al* (1999), Hillside, Norcross, Felix Holt and The Shire all failed to raise their measured effectiveness from one attainment level to the next.

Hillside's best GCSE 5A*- C percentage was achieved during the first year of the study, well before any improvement in effectiveness was reported. No upward trend emerged during the five years covered by the data, while annual fluctuations were within the range predicted on the basis of the percentage eligible for free meals (Ofsted, 1998:31). Mr. Turner worked hard at Norcross to apply the lessons of school effectiveness and made 'raising achievement' the central theme of his headship, but there was no performance gain beyond what might have been expected from FSM statistics. After an initial leap forward between 1990 and 1993, from a point well below the FSM predicted trend-line, Norcross consistently lagged behind local and national averages. Strategies adopted by the school to increase effectiveness, including action plans, target setting and performance monitoring seem to have added little to student attainment.

These disappointing, stable results are consistent with the growing evidence that very few schools produce a sustained improvement in student achievement, and that intake variables like social mix continue to account for most of the differences between schools (Levačić and Woods, 2002a, 2002b; Thrupp, 1999). Successive inspections at Norcross have noted the consequences of pit closure. The higher education uptake in the Norcross electoral ward is one of the lowest in the country. The government's own commissioned research emphasises the impact of disadvantage, finding that attainment is significantly below average in districts that 'have relatively high levels of deprivation'. Another report found that the dominant factors affecting performance in former coalfield areas are those associated with 'extreme social disadvantage' (DfES, 2001, 2003a).

Felix Holt and The Shire are situated in more prosperous districts than Hillside and Norcross, as the FSM statistics confirm (see Table 2, p92), and their headline performance figures give the impression of improved effectiveness. The percentage of students achieving 5 GCSE A*-C grades at Felix Holt rose during the period of the study from the mid-20s to the mid-50s, and at The Shire from the mid-40s to the mid-60s. Similar improvements are evident in the 16+ data. In both cases, however, the size and origin of the intake at 11+ and 16+ has altered so much that simple comparisons between past and present performance are of doubtful validity. The 50 per cent national increase in the number of students attaining 5 GCSE A*- C grades (between 1994 and 2008) further complicates the task of evaluating a school's progress over time.

Even so, there are important reasons for doubting whether these headline, unadjusted performance statistics should be interpreted as evidence of transformation leading to raised levels of effectiveness:

- GM and then specialist college status brought additional resources and enhanced competitiveness in the local education market (both schools)
- A better reputation earned access to more mobile and aspirational families (both schools)

■ Reported improvements in student intake and overall verbal reasoning scores contributed to better results (The Shire)

■ Ability to select up to 10 per cent of the intake assisted reputation and results (Felix Holt)

■ Results matched significantly below average FSM eligibility (both schools).

Once allowance is made for background variables, therefore, the available data at Felix Holt and The Shire seem to corroborate studies that have found transformative leadership has only a small, indirect impact on organisational effectiveness and outcomes (Hallinger and Heck, 1998).

This evidence is also consistent with other studies that question whether leadership impacts on school effectiveness. A survey of 3,500 Year-10 students and 2,500 of their teachers and principals in South Australia and Tasmania has led the authors to emphasise the inter-relationship of a wide range of variables and to doubt the more simple Hay/NCSL model of transformational leadership (Mulford, Silins and Leithwood, 2004). A recent study based on 20,000 students enrolled in 250 American schools has found that 'organic management,' including supportive leadership and staff collaboration, had no effect on 'achievement growth' (Miller and Rowan, 2006:242). The finding that organic management did not increase achievement for a very large number of US students explodes the 'strong claims' made about leadership and student outcomes. Can other effectiveness recommendations survive scrutiny like this? (Leithwood *et al*, 2006)

Relentless Pursuit of the Unattainable

These four case studies leave little doubt that leaders exert a profound influence and can bring about remarkable changes within a relatively brief period of time. The Hay/NCSL models explain in psychological terms how leaders impact on followers by creating a positive, motivational climate, and provide a useful descriptive framework for understanding and evaluating organisational change. Repeated observations of successful leaders have increased confidence in the government's transformative models, encouraging policy-makers and researchers to believe they have found a transferable formula or silver bullet that can be applied in any circumstances to improve quality and efficiency. Leaders seem able to transform 'ossified' social and organisational structures so that they become productive and successful, thereby squaring the circle of educational reform.

Unfortunately, the transformational benefits found in the case studies do not include the main purpose of school reform – improved effectiveness. Social disadvantage trumps leadership every time, so that remarkable, widely praised improvements have no more than a marginal influence on test and examination results. Even when outstanding heads follow the script to the letter, performance gains attributable to changes in school leadership are hard to trace, while the consequences of poverty in a school's intake remain obvious. The incidence of unemployment and the uptake of welfare benefits, including FSM, continue to provide a far more reliable guide to school performance than a head's LPSH diagnostic data. Despite the government's relentless pursuit of test and examination results, very few schools raise their effectiveness from one level to another. When results improve, the most likely explanation is that the school's intake has changed, due to an enhanced local reputation and middle class migration back in.

The relentless pursuit of improved effectiveness has failed, therefore, to secure its goal but has had other, unexpectedly negative consequences. Heads are not free to concentrate on transformational visions or independent missions for their apparently self-governing schools, but are compelled to adopt the definitions of quality and success imposed by the Performance Tables. Mr. Turner at Norcross saw no alternative but to implement short-term tactics designed to 'deliver' better results; Mr. Moore at Hillside ensured that every operation matched Ofsted requirements. Ms. Thomson at The Shire was committed to target setting, using data and benchmarks to monitor progress, while an outstanding English lesson at the school aimed to boost oral grades. An assistant head at Felix Holt was asked 'to make the data sing'. His teaching and learning reviews were based on value-added analysis, obliging heads of department to concentrate on raising the number of students achieving at least a GCSE grade C. This convergent, one-track approach is inconsistent with Bass's theory of transformational leadership, and is unlikely to generate conditions that inspire a genuine love of learning.

Another problem is that government agencies are obsessed with schools' examination performances and so overvalue personal leadership qualities that are supposed to contribute to league table success. As a result, other important dimensions of headship are neglected, including those relating to the moral and values basis of education. When there is little convincing evidence that leaders improve results, this emphasis on style and climate does not make sense. As the four case studies confirm, school leaders have to deal with a succession of intricate dilemmas about values and priorities that cannot be resolved by adopting a subtle blend of styles. There are infinite possible combinations of circumstances, values and interests, and these do not lend themselves to easy, one size fits all solutions. The rhetoric of reform masks the divergence between messianic government agencies pressing for improved test scores, and realistic school leaders dealing with the unpredictable complexity of organisational life.

A different approach is required if the potential role of leadership in bringing about improved learning is to be fully understood and realised. Leithwood and Levin (2005:4) believe we should also 'measure a more comprehensive set of leadership practices than has been included in most research to date' if we are to understand the varieties of school leadership that contribute most effectively to student progress. We need to explore how leaders contribute to a more broadly defined, qualitative conception of student development and outcomes beyond academic attainment.

6
Best Practice

Classroom Science

Government policies and agencies are orchestrated at every level to create the classroom conditions and 'behaviour for learning' believed to be necessary for a great increase in students' academic achievement. Policy-makers believe that 'we know what works' and do all they can to encourage schools and teachers, regardless of context, to implement a set of 'best practice' recommendations that are supposed to produce a major impact on effectiveness and performance. As we have seen, school leaders have been harnessed to a performance regime that has made them into 'bastard' managers, with an intense concentration on applying the lessons of classroom science to increase examination success. This chapter questions the government's assumption that researchers have identified the key school characteristics necessary for improved performance, and also challenges the claim that the hyper-accountability obsession has made classrooms more efficient and productive (Wright, 2001; Mansell, 2007).

Interest in classroom science is relatively recent in Britain, but the quest for organisational efficiency has been a continuing feature of American education for some considerable time. Since the days of Frederick 'Speedy' Taylor (1911), analogies with factory production have encouraged reformers to view schools and classrooms as facilities where scientific management can be applied to increase efficiency and output. The successful mass production techniques adopted in the US, particularly during World War 2, suggested that results could be greatly improved when intricate tasks demanding high levels of skill were sub-divided into standardised operations to be completed in a routine sequence. Schooling seemed to be another production process that could be accelerated and improved, so complex bureaucratic systems were devised to deliver learning and results as efficiently as possible. Despite major disappointments with large-scale Federal reform in the 1970s, classroom science has come into its own with the modern emphasis on competition and performance (Sarason, 1996).

Policy-makers hope that school leaders, like industrial managers, will introduce improved and more scientific methods. Like Weber (1964: 337), they believe technical knowledge is the 'primary source of the superiority of bureaucratic administration' and think of schools as pro-ductive units that should be adjusted to maximise the learning derived from a given volume of time and resources. Concerned with techniques that increase their own bureaucratic impact, officials are naturally dis-inclined to view teaching as a human art, like poetry, that cannot be cloned, standardised, mass-produced or otherwise subjected to mana-gerial manipulation. The result in the UK has been continued optimism about the benefits of a set of 'best practice' effectiveness recipes for teaching and school organisation.

The assumption that 'best practice' found at one location can be trans-ferred and applied in another, less successful context, so that eventually all schools become effective, is viewed as a fundamental, unproble-matic tenet of school reform. Government agencies have drawn on an extensive literature relating to school effectiveness to inform official recommendations about 'best practice' and assume that we 'know what works' in almost any circumstances (Gray *et al*, 1999; Luyten *et al*, 2005).

Table 3 presents the eleven key characteristics of effective schools found consistently in a wide range of studies across very different edu-cation systems. Successful, effective schools are believed to differ from schools in general in systematic and predictable ways that can be emulated (Wilson and Corcoran, 1988).

The DCSF, NCSL, Ofsted, and the TDA assume, therefore, that there is a clearly defined formula for academic success that can be applied any-where, regardless of the conditions, circumstances and issues that might influence a particular location. Ofsted have based their inspection

Effective School Factors

1 Professional leadership	Firm and purposeful
	A participative approach
	The leading professional
2 Shared vision and goals	Unity of purpose
	Consistency of practice
	Collegiality and collaboration
3 A learning environment	An orderly atmosphere
	An attractive working environment
4 Concentration on teaching and learning	Maximisation of learning time
	Academic emphasis
	Focus on achievement
5 Purposeful teaching	Efficient organisation
	Clarity of purpose
	Structured lessons
	Adaptive practice
6 High expectations	High expectations all round
	Communicating expectations
	Providing intellectual challenge
7 Positive reinforcement	Clear and fair discipline
	Feedback
8 Monitoring progress	Monitoring pupil performance
	Evaluating school performance
9 Pupil rights and responsibilities	Raising pupil self-esteem
	Positions of responsibility
	Control of work
10 Home-school partnership	Parental involvement in their children's learning
11 A learning organisation	School-based staff development

Table 3: Key Characteristics of Effective Schools (Sammons *et al*, 1995)

frameworks and recommendations on the international effectiveness research assembled by Sammons *et al* (1995). Schools have followed Ofsted instructions, introducing a range of effectiveness raising techniques that includes development and action planning, learning objectives and target-setting. Officials believe that behavioural regularities have been observed in successful institutions (e.g 'focus on achievement', 'high expectations', 'participative approach') and should be reproduced to secure improved performance. The conditions for effective learning can be prescribed and cloned. Strong leaders, driven by market competition and empowered by frequent Ofsted inspections, should challenge dysfunctional professional cultures and insist on rational, scientific practices that raise achievement and standards.

Schools as Systems

As policy-makers are concerned with general conditions rather than with local circumstances, they adopt rational, bureaucratic and rigid methods to ensure that schools implement best practice. Remote from the classroom action, interventionist officials and agencies are obliged to prescribe universally applicable, standardised rules, regulations, and recommendations. They have no alternative but to conceptualise the school as a system, and to influence its productive processes by changing the nature, quality and volume of inputs that it receives. Chart 3 shows this conception of the school as a system, open to influence through external inputs of various kinds.

Chart 3 represents a school system that receives inputs of children, books, materials, teachers, support staff and equipment. The government and various agencies intervene to ensure what they deem to be an appropriate mix and quality of inputs. They provide, for example, standards for teacher training and professional development, and have also negotiated a workforce agreement with unions to facilitate the effective deployment of personnel within the system (Stevenson, 2007b). The nature of the pupil intake is shaped by parental choice and established admissions criteria, while the resources for improved premises, equipment and materials depend on competitive success as well as the budgets assigned.

These inputs flow through the system, influencing in various ways the nature and quality of the leadership, classroom instruction and pastoral

Chart 3: School education viewed as a system (adapted from Deming, 1986, fig. 1, p4)

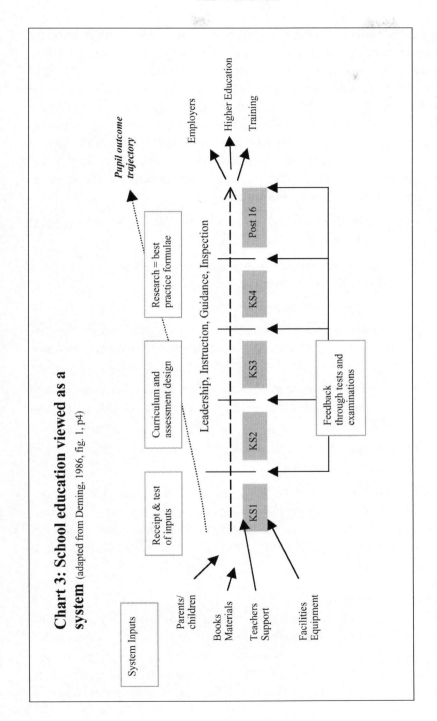

guidance provided. There is continuous feedback through tests and examinations at the end of each key stage (KS1, KS2 etc.), while Ofsted inspections check the system's efficiency and the quality of its output. Published performance tables enable schools to compare themselves with competitors and to identify and remedy weaknesses in their operations, including underachieving departments, teachers and students. The government further ensures system efficiency by continuously improving the standardised curriculum and assessment frameworks within which schools operate, and by making available the latest research into best practice techniques.

The assessment framework is essential to the operational management of the system because it:

- Enables the complex interactions of education to be measured and evaluated in standardised form

- Enables system goals and targets to be set

- Provides formative data about pupil progress and teacher performance for diagnostic purposes – the pupil outcome trajectory can be tracked to ensure that value is added

- Supplies summative data about system performance in relation to goals and targets (for the use of stakeholders and consumers)

- Assigns value to individual and system performance (through prescribed criteria).

Inputs can be adjusted to accommodate changing demands and circumstances, particularly when disappointing trends in the data signal the need for action or when employers, higher education representatives or training providers identify deficiencies in system outputs or products.

Effective Systems?

This portrayal of the school as a natural system, to be managed and directed according to objective, positivist and scientific principles, is apparently rational and appears to serve the purposes of government agencies set up to achieve well-defined and narrow goals. There are grounds, nevertheless, for honest doubt about the methods used to

manage the system, and about the dominant effectiveness recommendations applied to improve it.

Government agencies working to improve system inputs often adopt
coercive methods remote from their own recommendation that schools
should distribute leadership widely. Their strategies are the very opposite of those advised by management consultants and academics. In his
1986 book, *Out of the Crisis*, W. Edwards Deming wrote a 14-point wake-
up call for American companies that were then struggling to match
foreign competitors in terms of product cost and quality. He challenged
current practices, telling managers to eliminate the need for inspection
by designing quality into the product in the first place. He urged
companies to drive out people's fear of making a mistake, or not carry-
ing out instructions as directed, so that everyone felt able to contribute
positively.

Deming also demanded an end to slogans, targets for the workforce,
and exhortations to achieve new levels of productivity. These only
create negative reactions, he explained, because most of the causes of
low quality and low productivity originate with the system itself and are
beyond the control of the workforce. Deming insisted that management by objectives, management by numbers and the use of numerical
goals were harmful and should be eliminated from practice. UK officials
appear locked into pre-Deming mindsets and pursue their goals with
little concern for the impact on the system, on teachers and on students
(Deming, 1986).

This inept managerial approach compromises the success of school
reform but the government's excessive reliance on effectiveness research has also hindered progress.

The eleven key characteristics of effective schools capture in broad
terms a small number of factors that have been observed in schools
where students perform well in tests and examinations. Although
research data has consistently indicated an association between factors
and results, a causal relationship has not been established and there is
no theoretical basis for official models of effectiveness and improvement. On the contrary, no process or mechanism has been found to
explain how an individual, ineffective school can become effective. As
we have seen, one recent study of twelve improving schools, designed

to discover how they increased their effectiveness, found that none of the schools succeeded in making it from one level to the next. The researchers were frustrated by their realisation that: 'Differences between schools in their effectiveness simply swamped any changes in effectiveness (upwards or downwards)' (Gray *et al*, 1999:138). Effectiveness seems to be an intrinsic quality possessed by some schools with largely middle class intakes and not by others, with predominantly working class intakes, rather than a set of characteristics that can be acquired.

Recent studies do not suggest that particular methods or techniques are any more likely to produce guaranteed results than general recipes based on effectiveness research. Strong claims have been made, for example, about the gains that result when teaching is matched to a student's learning style. But Muijs *et al* (2005:60-2) found no difference in achievement between students 'whose instruction was matched, partially matched, or not matched to their learning style as measured using a learning styles inventory based on Kolb's work'. Stahl (1999) concludes that children's learning styles cannot be measured reliably. Gardner's (1993) theory of multiple intelligences has been promoted widely but the evidence so far is not supportive (Muijs *et al*, 2005).

Some research has found that methods that work for one topic are less successful for others. Varied pedagogy, for example, was less strongly related to gains in achievement in teaching number than in teaching calculation and measures, shape and space. Clear explanations and presentations, using a sufficiently long wait time after questions, using open ended questions, asking students to explain their answers and guiding students through the material were more strongly related to gains in measures, shape and space than in calculation (Muijs *et al*, 2005). The application of a general idea, like learning styles, didacticism or constructivism, seems less significant for learning than micro-level variations in context and the latent abilities of the children themselves (Gray *et al*, 1990). There does not seem to be a sure-fire formula to unlock potentially great leaps in learning for everyone. The relentless search for patterns of teacher behaviour that increase test scores has become counter-productive because it encourages schools to neglect other improvements that may be beneficial to the individual but are discounted because they are not perceived to enhance productivity.

Similar effectiveness propositions have crumbled when their supposed benefits have been subjected to detailed scrutiny (Luyten *et al*, 2005).

Animal Spirits

These negative conclusions suggest the limited usefulness of seeking a formative relationship between a small number of factors, especially when these are couched in ordinary, ambiguous language, and demonstrate how difficult it is to confirm a stable relationship between one variable and another in a closed system (e.g inside a school or classroom). The assumption that there is a performance formula that can be transferred from one site to another seems fundamentally flawed. Effectiveness recommendations depend on the belief that particular actions invariably produce the desired result, but in reality the variables within learning systems are highly irregular and non-linear, leading to context specific outcomes. Learning is not easily explained as the product of a simple combination of factors, and there is a tendency for officials and inspectors to under-estimate the complexity and inter-relationship of school variables and effects. Success is hard to account for and even harder to reproduce (Grace, 1998; Radford, 2006).

These problems, and the debate they provoke, are similar to those taking place in economics, where the 2008 crunch and crash have caused disillusionment with theories that failed to predict disaster. Akerlof and Shiller (2009) believe orthodox models were inadequate because of their misplaced confidence in human rationality, and a general reluctance to admit that human behaviour is strongly influenced by 'animal spirits'. Feelings, beliefs and story lines (e.g people are persuaded that 'boom and bust' economics have been replaced by managed growth) drive human action, but are omitted from standard theories that assume decisions are based on evidence and reasonable predictions. Akerlof and Shiller claim that no one predicted the fall of Lehman Brothers because economists paid too little attention to psychological factors and ignored the 'animal spirits' that were making Wall Street into an unregulated casino. Their aim is to improve economic theory so that it provides a more realistic basis for policy-making.

John Gray (2009) questions whether economists steeped in neo-liberal ideology will be interested in theories that emphasise the limits of rational action and the role of 'animal spirits'. Economists tend to see themselves as scientists, masters of mathematical formulae that enable predictions to be made and the future to be managed. Gray argues that this scientific self-conception is a mistake because: 'Economics and politics are not separate branches of human activity, and economic life cannot be studied independently of social divisions and political conflicts among populations, along with their cultures and religions'. Models of rational decision-making do not work, 'even when applied to the behaviour of markets' (2009:14).

This conclusion applies with equal strength to rational models of education, where the subjective values of the would-be scientists are equally intrusive and where human behaviour is even harder to manage and measure. A broader conception of education and society is needed than that provided by effectiveness models, with their intense, narrow but apparently rational concern for the annual progress of individual students and schools. Education and learning relate not only to particular people and institutions, but also to the structures in which they are situated, including their families, their communities and the society beyond, including the apparatus of the state itself. The intricate complexity of the phenomena and relationships involved are more visible when the reformer's lens is set to capture a richer, more human impression of the landscape, and suggest the limitations of research exploring factors and outcomes.

The essential problem is that students are not customers or clients whose minds are serviced and improved, but active organisation members who bring personality, interests, attitudes, cultural capital, and varying levels of ability to their formal and informal learning. These are the 'animal spirits' that transform learning, however scientific the teaching. Young people learn as much from their contemporaries as their teachers and their preferred curriculum extends beyond the school gate. Their individual minds and motives have been formed outside the system and respond in ways that are not easily observed or predicted. They are not all the same, with similar needs and aspirations. We need, therefore, to listen to teachers and students and their subjective perceptions if we are to improve our knowledge and understanding of schools as organisations (Greenfield and Ribbins, 1993).

An interpretive view of education provides, therefore, a critical alternative to the grand narrative of scientific reform. The interpretive position is based on the idea that successful learning depends on children's own subjective experience and perceptions, and on their need to connect the prescribed curriculum with everyday life. Learners need to relate new knowledge and impressions to their existing thoughts and feelings. Test knowledge is imperfectly learned and soon forgotten, therefore, partly because it is perceived as lacking relevance, but also because learning for tests is often mnemonic, concerned with accurate repetition and reproduction rather than with personal growth, and is communicated by methods that do not engage the heart or mind, beyond the immediate purpose of securing a respectable examination result.

Defining and Measuring Progress

The assessment apparatus developed since the 1988 Reform Act is entirely positivist in conception and operation, however, and plays a central role in managing and improving the system. It generates the data used to define and measure children's learning and progress, and to evaluate school and teacher effectiveness. Performance data is also the foundation for effectiveness research and so forms our understanding of 'what works' and helps identify the best practice schools should emulate. The resulting assumptions are tautological. Effective schools are those that achieve better test and examination results.

Using results as the prime measure of a successful education within a well-defined framework of accountability seems rational and value-neutral. Annual cycles produce a wealth of statistics that enable managers at all levels to set targets, measure progress and judge institutional effectiveness. Policy-makers are convinced they have devised a reliable accountability system to drive up standards, and employ every device imaginable to ensure that students and teachers are fully mobilised in a ceaseless quest for better grades. School reform stands or falls, therefore, by the reliability of the statistical information that emerges from the system, and by the validity of that data as an accurate indicator of educational quality (Ball, 2003b; Twelftree, 2007).

The dominance of the performance regime has masked, nevertheless, the extent to which official curriculum requirements, and the selected measures of success (e.g the five A*-C GCSE grades threshold), have distorted and changed the nature of education. Schools teach to the test, choose examinations with the best chance of a higher grade (e.g General National Vocational Qualifications (GNVQ)), reduce the time devoted to non-examinable activities and concentrate attention on borderline candidates (Gray *et al*, 1999; McNeil, 2000; Mansell, 2007). The contested, political origins of the National Curriculum are now forgotten, but the consequences of its distinctive bias are under-estimated. The standardised model that prevailed in 1988 was not a wise and rational distillation of human knowledge but a ruthless restoration of the traditional priorities believed to have been threatened by the progressive experiments of the 1960s and 1970s. The National Curriculum aimed to control teachers' work and so discouraged local initiative and innovation (Simon, 1988; Apple, 1989; Chitty, 1989).

The regulations prescribed, therefore, an overwhelmingly academic diet that fails to meet the needs of many students. Since then, policy has emphasised the value of the managerially 'effective' and has ignored the creative, expressive and affective aspects of learning and teaching (McNess *et al*, 2003). This curriculum bias is reinforced by level descriptors that characterise the skills and abilities expected of students at each age and key stage (Sainsbury and Sizmur, 1998). The eight levels describe an incremental, linear progression through ever more conceptually demanding activities. This rewards intelligent individuals whose families have transmitted the ability to cope with complex language and abstract ideas. Meanwhile, 'the educational mortality rate can only increase as one moves towards the classes most distant from scholarly language' (Passeron 1990:73).

Put more simply, the curriculum is designed mainly for those with high verbal reasoning scores and therefore leaves many unable to improve beyond a well-defined cognitive ceiling. Whatever their experience, practical skill and personal development, many below average students find themselves negatively labelled and stuck permanently, unable to progress through the abstract concepts and technical accomplishments covered by the higher level descriptors. The latest QCA attainment target descriptors in English, for example, include this expectation of written performance at level 5:

Pupils' writing is varied and interesting, conveying meaning clearly in a range of forms for different readers, using a more formal style where appropriate. Vocabulary choices are imaginative and words are used precisely. Sentences, including complex ones, and paragraphs are coherent, clear and well developed. Words with complex regular patterns are usually spelt correctly. A range of punctuation, including commas, apostrophes and inverted commas, is usually used accurately. Handwriting is joined, clear and fluent and, where appropriate, is adapted to a range of tasks. (QCA, 2007b:80; Attainment Target 3: Writing)

This target requires a level of technical skill that is likely to remain beyond the reach of many ordinary and disadvantaged children. Progress is defined so that personal experience and growth are excluded, unless they can be expressed within the formal technical requirements of the narrow and prescriptive assessment framework.

On the other hand, the latest version of the National Curriculum promises that schools will have greater flexibility and coherence, scope for personalisation and more opportunities for links with the wider curriculum (QCA, 2007a). This is another sign that government agencies have begun to recognise the limitations of the 'command and control' curriculum regime and is evidence of a new policy direction that should be encouraged and continued.

The performance tables continue to promote, nevertheless, a distinctive, unacknowledged set of values. Certain abilities and skills are recognised while others are not. The aura of public information legitimises the use of carefully selected statistics to promote aggressively competitive and individualist values. Celebrations of successful schools are supposed to encourage improvement for the disadvantaged but the annual ritual in fact repeatedly demonstrates the raw incompatibility of excellence and inclusion. The more poor children you happen to teach, the less well you and your school will do.

The performance system is also misleading. Schools and teachers are recognised as valuable only when students achieve 'better than expected' results. They play an essential, formative role through their students' learning journeys but the 'value added' contribution is calculated only in terms of the margin of difference between actual and anticipated test or examination scores. Teachers may radically change and enrich children's lives but their influence does not count in the hyper-accountability stakes unless the results exceed expectations. The continuous interplay between students, schools, families, and communities is therefore discounted or at least undervalued, unless the numerical data is consistently better than elsewhere.

Above all, the performance arrangements, with their strange trust in unadjusted data, are invalid, unreliable and often misleading (Goldstein and Thomas, 1996; Goldstein, 2001). During 20 years of compulsive reform since 1988, key stage tests, GCSE examinations and A levels have become chronically unstable. Constant changes have undermined the basis for comparisons over time (West and Pennell, 2000; Goldstein, 2001; ASCL, 2008). How should reported achievements in language and number be assessed, for example, when we know that progress is measured only in relation to the current government's period in office? Should we trust the claims of ministers who have almost total control over what is learned and assessed (Smithers, 2007)? Official statistics no longer command automatic trust and respect but the whole system is driven, nevertheless, by the annual cycle of target setting and results (Goldstein and Spiegelhalter, 1996). The data system is, therefore, not fit for purpose.

English education seems obsessed with defying the laws of statistical gravity, but does not acknowledge the likely outcome. Tests and examinations are valued because they discriminate between pupils. When they cease to perform this function, they become discredited and are eventually replaced by a more convincing and competitive alternative. Prizes lose their value when everyone wins them.

Teaching to the Test
The classroom level impact of the effectiveness regime is not easily assessed because individual schools and teachers, influenced by different sets of local conditions, respond in contrasting ways to the same external stimuli. Some heads are wary of the enemy at the gate, particularly when their performance data places them in a vulnerable category. Other school leaders take pleasure in their managerial skills and ability to 'play the game'.

116

The policy sociologist Stephen Ball is convinced, nevertheless, that the techniques intended to increase performance and effectiveness produce instead a culture or system of terror in schools. School leaders become enforcers, assisting in the work of audit and inspection, while the teachers themselves teach to tests that have little connection with a quest for knowledge. The result is emotional pressure and stress; a relentless intensification of work that overspills into private life; increased competition within and between institutions; mutual surveillance; and bureaucratic paperwork that diverts everyone from the real business of working with children (2003b, 2008).

There is disturbing evidence that Ball may be right about the terror. Each year, between 600 and 800 people under the age of 24 in the UK take their own lives (Parkinson, 2006:1). As many as 24,000 young people between the ages of 10 and 19 are believed to attempt suicide each year and one in ten have been found to self-harm as a way of coping with stress. Boys and girls feel that there is a huge amount of pressure to do well and claim that homework and increased school workloads, including coursework, are their biggest source of stress (Schmidt, 2007). Anne Parry, chair of Papyrus, a charity committed to preventing young suicides, believes that for many students exam pressures can be overwhelming:

> We sometimes hear a story of a young person who has taken his or her life after their university exams, some when they have gained an upper-second-class degree rather than a first. Don't pressure young people, particularly if you know that they're conscientious anyway. Encourage them to take time out. We mislead young people into thinking the only way forward in life is to get good GCSEs, A-levels and then a degree. That's not the case (Parkinson, 2006:1).

Government agencies have deliberately increased the competitive pressure to which schools and children are subjected, so this evidence of stress and anxiety is less than surprising. Drive people hard and some will crack. Anne Parry is not alone, however, in asking whether the pressure is aimed at the right target or produces the desired result. Capable and conscientious students do their best in any system, while less capable and less conscientious individuals find ways to detach themselves from unequal competitions that offer no reward. Is the textbook learning forced into young people's short-term memories worth the pain? Does cramming for exams produce lasting benefits?

Hoyle and Wallace (2007) argue that the pressure and stress are in vain. They find irony and pathos in a scientific system driven by the pursuit of the impossible. They argue that the top down reform model creates an implementation gap between the intentions of the policymakers and their interpretation in schools and classrooms. A ceaseless flow of initiatives is implemented through Chinese whispers. Teachers do not own reform and wait to be told what to do, or engage in quiet subversion and resistance. As a result, educational goals are not agreed or shared. Reform is subject, therefore, to an endemic and fatal irony.

Empirical evidence confirms this interpretation. Over a period of years, the cumulative effect of the five reform propositions outlined in chapter 1 has been to convert previously diverse teaching styles and methods into the technocratic pursuit of the one, right answer. Held accountable for student results in twenty different ways, including the arrangements for performance pay, teachers teach to the test and ensure their pupils are drilled to produce the required response. Coursework provides obvious opportunities to improve students' grades. Michelle Ford's food technology students, for example, have their GCSE coursework covered with sticky labels. As she explained to Warwick Mansell, a visiting journalist from the *Times Educational Supplement*, the labels tell class members what to write.

When the files are marked, the stickers are removed so there is no evidence of cheating should the work be sent to the examination board for checking. The written guidance on the stickers more or less guarantees her pupils a good grade every year. This produces an excellent value added result, even though it means class members gain good grades without any independent thought. Although Michelle was more open about her exam-busting techniques than other teachers, Mansell is sure that her approach is symptomatic of a general abuse of in-class assessment, mostly caused by the demands of hyper-accountability (Mansell, 2007).

Teachers are also eager to help students give the right answers in written examinations. Mansell (2007) visited a class for fourteen year olds at a Yorkshire comprehensive. The lesson appeared to be about

Michael Morpurgo's *Private Peaceful,* a story that culminates in the trenches on the Western front and includes a vivid account of a gas attack. The pupils were not asked to reflect on the Somme tragedy or the quality of Morpurgo's writing, however. Instead, the story was used as an exercise. Students were asked to review sample answers to test-type questions and to consider the features that would earn the most marks. The teacher did not discuss the author's skill or the virtues of the story but asked the class to identify three strengths and three weaknesses in the sample answers. Mansell's conclusion is that: 'Many secondary schools, in their desperation to improve results, are being encouraged to reduce literature study to anodyne exercises such as the one above in how to please the examiner, turning young people away from a love of books' (Mansell, 2007:53-54).

Linda McNeil's (2000) study of 'magnet' schools also found that an emphasis on test performance produces a compliance culture devoted to results. Standardised reforms in Texas forced the best teachers to water down their content so that computers could mark the answers. There was a marked shift away from intellectual activity towards dispensing packaged fragments of information. The Houston 'magnet' schools, set up initially to create learning opportunities for the disadvantaged, were regulated to narrow the curriculum and de-skill teachers. Performance pay encouraged 'pedagogical gamesmanship', while standardised tests excluded the personal and professional knowledge that had previously contributed to innovative teaching. McNeil found that teachers and students reacted against imposed controls by limiting their work. Schools and teachers were expected to prove their competence through improved test results. At one school, students were found to practice 'five paragraph' essays every day and to devote much of their time to test preparation.

Tests and examinations are supposed to create opportunities for everyone to succeed but in reality large cohorts of average and below average children experience routine failure that damages their sense of their own worth and efficacy. Children have an uncanny knowledge of where they stand in relation to their peers, even when grade boundaries are manipulated to create the illusion of better results. As 'ordinary kids' absorb discouraging assignment marks, disappointing practice grades and dispiriting examination results through their long years at school, they learn they have been left behind in a race played by alien rules. Since 1988, the high-stakes test regime has increased their sense of failure and encourages them to think of school as 'a place where they make you go and where they tell you to do things and where they try to make your life unpleasant if you don't do them right' (Holt, 1964:47). Average and below average students are obliged to participate in intense written competitions that are supposed to provide scope for social mobility but in reality validate and confirm pre-existing status positions.

Even at very good schools, in exciting lessons, the preoccupation with results demands that teachers concentrate on maximising grades rather than ensuring the quality of learning. At The Shire School, found by Ofsted to be 'very good and extremely effective', the real purpose of an excellent lesson was to create opportunities for the teacher to record good oral grades. Students from Year 11, equipped with prepared poems and carefully planned learning activities, worked in groups with Year 7 children. The two sets of young people were given name badges, were introduced to one another, and quickly generated a steady buzz of explanation and discussion about a wide variety of poems. The teacher moved between tables with a clipboard, recording oral contributions but also pausing to explain the difference between a simile and a metaphor. She commented that the format had created 'so many opportunities to score points ... their oral grades have rocketed up' (quoted in Barker, 2007:34).

Concentration on grades reduces the time available for activity that does not contribute to a student's ability to 'score points'. As McNeil (2000) discovered, once payment by results was introduced, her Houston teachers ceased to talk about their personal knowledge and experience, and discouraged their students from exploring topics that were not strictly relevant to the set task. Discursive discussion and debate are closed down as 'irrelevant' and time-consuming. Teaching to the test has become the main characteristic of the reformed, payment by results, classroom.

Wynne Harlen's report on primary science further confirms the pervasiveness of test culture. She argues that the negative impact on learning is not derived from the assessment process as such, but follows from the policy of using results to set targets and judge teachers and schools. The report includes three clear recommendations:

- 'National tests should be replaced by moderated teachers' assessment, so that progress in the full range of skills and concepts can be recorded and reported.

- There should be no high-stakes use of summative assessment of pupils' progress at the primary level as this distorts teaching and learning.

- Schools' provision for primary pupils' learning in science should be evaluated against a wide range of indicators of quality, of which the levels of pupils' achievement would be only one.' (Harlen, 2008:16)

The obsession with results as a surrogate for standards is so intense that hyper-accountability has become deeply entrenched in schools and classrooms. School leaders and teachers are made compliant by the primitive but effective psychological trick of Ofsted punishment and performance pay reward. Politicians have adopted, however, a messianic, persuasive language of vision and transformation that thinly masks the dismal reality. Although government agencies are devoted to a single goal – increasing the number of children with results matching specified criteria – Tony Blair made his education project sound much more broad and attractive: 'So our task now is to transform our secondary schools. That transformation will be achieved only by the creativity, dedication and vision of our head teachers, the new social entrepreneurs' (2001:22).

When the NCSL was launched in 2002 with a budget of £60 million per year, the Secretary of State announced that it would 'play a key role in the Government's strategy to transform our schools, drive up standards and ensure that every school is excellent or improving or both' (Blunkett, 2000:1). In reality, however, the education system has become obsessed by examination results and is transformed only in the sense that grades and numbers dominate the landscape.

Strangled Alternatives
The role of Ofsted in producing compliant classrooms obsessed with data should not be under-estimated. Regular inspections have induced

fear and shame in many less successful schools, and have obliged teachers everywhere to follow an agenda that makes them uncertain and insecure. Professor Ted Wragg wrote many articles indicting the bureaucratic, coercive methods adopted by government agencies and was an early critic of an inspection regime based on examination results:

> The policy adopted by the Government and its agencies is presumably founded on the belief that professional people are best motivated by threat and criticism ... The 'blame and shame' school of educational management has been most clearly implemented in three closely linked forms: (1) a mechanical style of school inspection, (2) a narrowly focused programme of national testing, and (3) the use of league tables to encourage schools to improve their performance. (Wragg, 1997:2)

At Hillside, a geography teacher wept when talking about her experiences illustrating the personal cost of 'blame and shame' methods:

> I've not got over it, I'm sure they said positive things but she destroyed me, I've lost all my confidence, I doubt what I'm doing, I thought it was alright; I know I've got problems ... I can get going, but if they won't learn I can't handle it; she (the Ofsted inspector) said they weren't making progress, I've lost my way. (quoted in Barker, 2003:123)

Teachers observed working in similar conditions in the US kept two sets of books:

> They keep a close eye on what others expect of them: prescribed curricula, minimum student competencies, criteria against which they will be evaluated. They may appear to meet the specifications of these external lists. They also keep a careful eye on what they want to accomplish in their work, according to their own version of a good school or classroom. Unfortunately, the dissonance and exhaustion created by merely living with, much less reconciling, these two sets of books too often obliterate any good that might be inherent in either. (Barth, 1990:40/41)

As the standards and accountability regime has matured, its narrowly economic, labour market conception of education has become transparent and teachers have found it ever more difficult to believe in what is required of them. School leaders have been reluctant, however, to pursue alternative visions. This is partly because the dominant narrative emphasises business-like efficiency and scorns educational outcomes that cannot be measured in numbers, but also because Ofsted inspectors police the system to ensure convergence, compliance and submission. There seems to be no escape.

Casablanca

This generally pessimistic conclusion may underestimate the ability of intelligent people to transcend the constraints that seem to govern them. The making of the film *Casablanca* shows that a masterpiece can emerge from the most unlikely circumstances and that rigorous accountability need not destroy creativity. Maurice Holt identifies 'similarities between the work of schools and the work of movie-making under the studio system', particularly in terms of their management and creative processes. This 1942 Warner Brothers' film was a low budget production aimed at a captive audience eager for romance, but determined managers found ways to make the movie a timeless classic despite the circumstances (Holt, 1996:249).

As studio head, Jack Warner could interfere as much as he pleased, but shifted his ground when Hal Wallis took over as producer. There was a 'loose coupling' between tough accountability and a creative climate that enabled Wallis to adopt a naturalistic approach to problems and opportunities. Ingrid Bergman was available if shooting started immediately. Wallis took the chance and set the cameras rolling. The film's making was 'woefully unplanned', with scenes shot out of sequence and constant changes in the script. But *Casablanca* is a classic, nevertheless, because Wallis got the best out of his chosen director and team. Their practical solutions worked. According to Holt: '*Casablanca* exemplifies the virtues of focusing on process – on the dilemmas of narrative – and bringing the talents of everyone to bear on the task of resolving them' (1996:251). The making of the film suggests, therefore, that even in conditions of mass production, tight budgets and hyper-accountability, skilled managers and their staff can produce memorable, unique and high quality work. Although the hyper-accountability regime produces difficult classroom conditions for teachers who do not believe in education by numbers, imaginative work may still be possible. There may be more scope for teacher agency than we expect, given the government's high-pressure agenda. Even in bleak times, schools remain places of great energy and possibility.

Slow Learning

The performance regime is dominant, nevertheless, and has created conditions that leave remarkably little space for alternatives. Gareth Malone's choir at Lancaster Boys' School may have succeeded in unlikely circumstances but the government and its agencies have worked hard to produce an environment that rewards only academic priorities. Creative teachers and students have to work against the grain and their instinctively divergent thinking is ill adapted to the world of self-evaluation forms and value-added calculations.

The essential weakness of official recommendations is that they are concerned with immediate, short-term objectives that have little meaning for teachers and children beyond the obvious satisfaction of achieving good grades. What can we do to accelerate learning? How do we get the results up? Government agencies think of learning as a progressive sequence, with each step located in moments of acquisition and practice. After thirty minutes observing a classroom, Ofsted inspectors believe they have sufficient data to make pronouncements about the simultaneous progress of up to 30 people and to judge the effectiveness of the teacher. The current emphasis on written examinations encourages the idea that learning happens within a limited period of time and that its quality can be captured in a pencil and paper test. Policymakers and their agents are strangely reluctant to acknowledge that learning extends beyond the eye of the observer and involves a complex process of internal growth that may take many years.

Our son's work on Robin Hood's Bay illustrates this phenomenon. As a ten year old, he spent a week in Scarborough with his primary school and enjoyed a day out in Robin Hood's Bay. Back at school, he was asked to remember the scene. His stitched landscape is pinned to our kitchen wall to this day. As a 19 year old, he returned home from York University, where he was studying Biology, and showed us this poem:

Robin Hood's Bay

My favourite thing was sewing,
Stitching Robin Hood's bay in cloth.

(not embroidery – that was for girls)

Sea weed from old tights,
teacher's proud display.

Lady mayor tickled
(displayed at the town hall)
by my use of blue silk for sea.

I finished maths fast,
Stitched during assembly
(special permission)
Rocks stuffed with foam.
Seagulls cut from linen,
Flew above my hessian sand.

Aged 7 I thought it was brilliant.

(but it wasn't)

When teachers planned the annual journey to Scarborough, they were guided by an intuitive sense that outdoor experiences stimulate children. They arranged to visit a dramatic natural landscape and back at school provided time and materials to enable the young travellers to remember and express what they had seen, heard and felt. As the children began to sew, the project took on a life of its own, with usual school routines suspended so their work could be finished in time for display at the town hall. Our son was obviously pleased and quietly amused when he was allowed ('special permission') to finish maths fast, and to stitch during assembly.

Ten years later, his early perceptions have morphed into an affectionate, gently ironic memory of a sewing project that caught and held his imagination long afterwards. He writes through the eyes of his younger self ('rocks stuffed with foam'), and is wistfully amused by his own qualified innocence ('that was for girls'). His learning about sewing, wild places, teachers, mayors, and his own innocence and experience, seems to have circled round in his mind for years, like the seagulls flying in the wind 'above my hessian sand'. His teachers never saw his poem, nor knew the long after-life of their work, partly because the display in the town hall was the end for the sewing project, and partly because learning, like memory, evolves unseen and unheard, with incalculable results.

Conceived as an inner, hidden, slowly growing, unpredictable mixture of thought and experience, this learning is quite different from the standardised, packaged, sequenced, time-bound acquisition of knowledge and skills envisaged by the National Curriculum and its associated assessment arrangements. Maurice Holt suggests that the concept of Slow, as it has emerged from the Slow Food movement, provides a culinary metaphor to help us interpret the contrast between the fast, 'standards-based school curriculum, with its emphasis on regurgitated gobbets of knowledge', and slow institutions 'where students have time to discuss, argue, and reflect upon knowledge and ideas, and so come to understand themselves and the culture they will inherit'. Holt claims that compared with slowly cooked food, prepared with respect for its ingredients, 'a burger has little nutritional value' (2002a, 2002b:1/2).

As the pendulum swings against the performance regime, we need to concentrate on this fundamentally different conception of learning, and to consider how to create the policy conditions that place all elements of children's growth, not just their examination achievements, at the centre of school life.

7

Progressive Alternatives

Progressive Comprehensives

This chapter draws on progressive ideas about young people's subjective needs, experiences and perceptions to challenge the validity and usefulness of the five reform propositions discussed in chapters 2-6, and seeks to establish firm foundations for a transformed approach to education policy. Once the progressive insistence on the importance of children's subjective construction of experience is acknowledged, the limitations of rational models of schooling are exposed. As the pendulum swings, policy-makers and their advisers have a new moral imperative – to recognise, to understand and to work with the knowledge that each child's learning represents a personal journey through myriad experiences, guided by cultural assumptions and theories-in-use rather than by interacting factors adjusted and managed by bureaucrats who know nothing of their lives.

The leaders of the early, 1960s comprehensives, especially those with a background in progressive education, understood the harmful consequences of competitive individualism, especially for less successful members of society. As pioneers of the common school, they aimed to forge inclusive social institutions, where students would be valued equally, and were determined that the new all-ability schools should be democratic communities, rather than sorting machines for the labour market. They were deeply committed to social justice and working class education, and believed that everyone could learn and succeed, whatever their social origins and disadvantages. Caroline Benn, Brian Simon and other campaigners for comprehensive education were convinced that all-ability schools, based on democratic, progressive principles, would produce self-confident citizens for a more equal, fair and socially just society.

Despite New Labour's transparent failure to improve the prospects of disadvantaged children, contemporary discourse allows little space for such alternative policies. The elaborate, top-down architecture of market-based reform established since 1988 is seen as the essential guarantee of quality and standards, although no one really believes that children's reading, writing and arithmetic have improved much in recent years. Disappointed by failure, policy analysts are disposed to blame teachers for not responding with sufficient enthusiasm, and propose yet more reform. Even so, the progressive critique of didactic teaching, academic curriculum structures and inappropriate examinations is apposite and applicable today, because, as we have seen, the hyper-accountability regime has encouraged a narrow and unproductive approach to learning. There is, however, a deep reluctance to remember and draw upon progressive insights that might threaten the narrative of markets and standards (Apple, 2004).

Neo-liberal ideologists have successfully constructed an imaginary past when comprehensive teachers failed their pupils by adopting a carelessly permissive attitude towards behaviour and examination results. After the Auld Report (1976) documented the apparent failure of progressive methods at a north London primary school, the innovations of the 1960s and 1970s were stigmatised as the work of subversives and lunatics who were supposed to have betrayed a generation of working class children by neglecting the basics. Whatever the truth, progressive and democratic models of schooling are now seen as engines of chaos, and standardised national templates have been imposed so that children are never again threatened by the dangerous dreams and ideologies of egalitarian educators.

During the 1960s and 1970s, however, comprehensive schools confronted the difficulties of educating the full ability range in a class divided society, and learned first-hand the limitations of traditional practices (e.g streaming, didactic teaching, corporal punishment) that made schools brutal environments for many low status children.

Thoughtful teachers, influenced by these experiences, and attracted by progressive ideas, began to develop a new, idealistic vision of comprehensive education that remains relevant today.

Tim McMullen (1968), first principal of Countesthorpe Community College in Leicestershire, was a radical who believed that something new and different was needed if children of all abilities were to become effective members of a democratic society. He was forthright in declaring that in any establishment for which he was responsible the school and community would be one unit, and the whole academic emphasis would be on children learning rather than teachers teaching. Children should be motivated as much by their natural curiosity and creativity as by the prospect of ever-increasing examination and career success.

Michael Duane (at Rising Hill) and Robert Mackenzie (at Summerhill Academy) became legendary prophets as advocates of progressive methods in state education. Influenced by European child-centred ideas, they emphasised freedom for children to develop in a loving and caring environment, where learning by discovery was the key to improving their self-belief and knowledge. Mackenzie questioned the state of Scottish education at that time, arguing that it was stultified by an over-reliance on out-dated methods and repetitive memory work. The curriculum was dominated by examinations and life skills were neglected (Berg, 1968; Murphy, 2007). In England, the Sutton Centre in Nottinghamshire aroused fierce controversy when it was announced that there would be no setting or streaming, and no preparation for GCE Ordinary level. Instead, all pupils would work towards the teacher controlled Mode III Certificate in Secondary Education (CSE) (Fletcher *et al*, 1985).

These innovations were an imaginative response to contemporary educational and social structures that restricted opportunity and success, particularly for ordinary people. It is absurd now to accuse these early comprehensive heads and teachers of letting their students down by neglecting achievement when the whole system in those days impeded access and rationed award-bearing courses. The school leaving age (not raised from 15 to 16 until 1974) ensured that large numbers of grammar, secondary modern and comprehensive graduates left without worthwhile qualifications, while the divided GCE/CSE examination structures (not reformed until 1986) were poorly adapted to the needs of the full ability range they were expected to serve. Only five per cent of students from manual occupational backgrounds received higher education in 1970, compared with over 30 per cent from non-manual backgrounds (DfES, 2003b).

The first comprehensives were determined, therefore, to improve their students' life chances, but found themselves operating within a divided education system that offered average and disadvantaged students little scope for tangible academic achievement. British education and society were bedevilled by inequality and unfairness, and progressive comprehensive schools were in the vanguard of those pressing for everyone to have access to opportunities once the preserve of the middle class. Labour's return to power in October 1964 rapidly increased the size and immediacy of this threat to the established order. Michael Stewart, the new Secretary of State, announced in November that the government's policy was 'to reorganise secondary education on comprehensive lines' (quoted in Simon, 1991:276).

The vitriolic nature of the assault on a handful of explicitly progressive schools reveals the extent to which entrenched interests felt threatened by the comprehensive challenge (Simon, 1991). The first Black Paper (Cox and Dyson, 1969) attacked the disastrous consequences of progressive education at a time when very few local authorities had reorganised 'on comprehensive lines' and when only a tiny number of schools had begun to experiment with child-centred methods. John Watts, who replaced McMullen as head of Countesthorpe in 1972, acknowledged that you would soon run into trouble if you encouraged students to question tradition and take control of their own destinies. He believed that progressives were bound to meet conflict with an industrial society where dominant groups saw schools as 'the sorting house for employment' (Fletcher et al, 1985).

The attack on teachers who aimed to 'question assumptions' and to 'envisage speculative alternatives' was intense. Rising Hill, Countesthorpe and Sutton Centre in England, and Summerhill Academy in Scotland, became 'Schools on Trial' after public controversy over their progressive methods. The schools were martyred in a media storm and their heads were driven out (Fletcher et al, 1985).

The Progressive Inheritance

These leading radicals combined progressive insights with their own experience to analyse the problems comprehensives would have to overcome. Their practical intelligence pointed them towards the organisational, curriculum and pedagogical changes necessary for inclusive schooling. Media hostility, at the time and since, has not reduced the validity of their critique of traditional education. Inequality between children was and remains an inescapable reality for all-ability schools. Streaming by ability tended and still tends to place students according to their class origins. The heterogeneous clients of the new all-ability schools would test traditional academic subjects to near destruction, and demonstrate the acute need to take account of children's experience and interests in planning the curriculum. The unreformed GCE examinations blocked innovation and rewarded traditional, memory-based teaching.

Progressive innovators followed John Dewey (1897) in emphasising children's activity and engagement, and saw A.S. Neill (1962), the head of Summerhill, a famous residential independent school, as an important campaigner against traditional conceptions of learning. Henry Morris, the innovator of the Cambridgeshire village colleges, was almost as important in influencing their thinking about the relationship between school and community. Impington Village College, designed by Walter Gropius and opened in 1939, gave architectural expression to the idea that education and the community were essential to one another. Morris (1925) believed that his village colleges should:

> ...provide for the whole man (*sic*), and abolish the duality of education and ordinary life. It would not only be the training ground for the art of living, but the place in which life is lived, the environment of a genuine corporate life.

John Watts, who taught at Sawston, the first Cambridgeshire village college, from 1953 to 1958, was convinced that the new comprehensives should be at the heart of their communities, as a source of social inclusion and lifelong learning, and should be a counterweight to the individualism and fragmentation of modern life. Countesthorpe, where Watts was principal from 1972 to 1980, was one of several comprehensive upper schools in Leicestershire that aimed to forge an identity based on new, positive relationships between adults and adolescents, new curriculum structures, and student-centred learning methods (Davies, 2009).

131

Progressive comprehensives also emphasised social integration through their internal organisation. Upper, middle and lower streams were replaced by mixed ability forms, with some limited subject setting. Authority was played down, while democracy and community were talked up. Corporal punishment was abolished, partly through a principled rejection of violence, but also because the cane and the tawse were symbols of what was wrong with traditional relationships between students and teachers. CSE Mode III examinations were introduced to create the space for flexible, school-based curriculum development. Above all, progressives stressed the importance of recognising and nurturing the child's natural curiosity and desire to learn. Teachers should create conditions where students were enabled to explore the world around them, rather than impose adult structures of thought and knowledge.

These solutions recognised the reality of children's lives and the obstacles to their learning. They also challenged prevailing modes of school and classroom organisation that tended to reduce engagement and motivation. Although innovation was often prompted by concern for disadvantaged working class children, the underlying progressive agenda was believed to be equally relevant and appropriate for everyone at school. Heads like McMullen, Watts, Duane and Mackenzie, influenced by the egalitarian legacy of the 1940s and aware of the many enduring obstacles to learning, were passionately eager to transform society. They were visionaries who attempted a unique reconstruction of state schooling from the inside.

The progressive programme of the late 1960s and early 1970s was, however, startlingly ambitious and was implemented with extraordinary naïveté. Lawrence Stenhouse (1969), for example, wrote about the Humanities Curriculum Project as if established power relations and old-fashioned classroom practices would melt away when his new scheme and its benefits were properly understood:

> This new pattern of teaching radically changes teacher-pupil relationships and has profound implications for the authority structure of the school. Schools are not likely to succeed in the changeover if they won't face a move from authoritarianism.

Since those optimistic days, we have learned from Seymour Sarason (1996) that the 'culture of the school' is resistant to change, so much so that most reform initiatives fail. Brought up and trained in traditional schools, and accustomed to dominating their classrooms, few teachers at the time were prepared to understand or implement progressive methods or to surrender their own classroom based power and control. Although the 1960s and 1970s are remembered for reckless experiments, there were in reality remarkably few schools or teachers ready to embrace Utopia. In retrospect, Michael Duane and Robert Mackenzie seem hapless innocents wandering in a jungle of wild beasts (Berg, 1968).

Blissfully unaware of the principles of change management, they simply announced the end of corporal punishment in their schools, without troubling to persuade their colleagues or to build support in their communities for an abrupt change of practice (Limond, 2005; Murphy, 2007). Tim McMullen was no more successful in securing support for his radical plans at Countesthorpe and had departed the school by 1972. As he became more committed to progressive practices, he grew less concerned with the public reaction. These hero-innovators adopted challenging management styles that were sometimes less than consistent with progressive goals, and reacted to opposition in ways that contributed to their own downfall (Fletcher *et al*, 1985).

The media-led stereotyping of progressive teaching as a madcap exercise in liberty and chaos was part of a wider cultural shift that contributed to the neo-liberal ascendancy under Thatcher in the UK and Reagan in the US. Progressive educators were misrepresented or even libelled[12] while their critical insights were discounted and ignored. Markets became the solution to every problem and progressive concerns were erased from the policy agenda. Poverty was denied; inequality was actively promoted; competitive individualism was encouraged. An imposed curriculum and testing regime consigned disadvantaged children to the inevitability of boredom followed by failure (Apple, 2004).

The 1960s progressives succeeded, nevertheless, in identifying fundamental flaws in traditional education. Almost forty years later, after immense social and economic changes, that include the near-disappearance of the skilled working class (Bunting, 2009), the essential problems identified in the early days of the comprehensive movement remain. The five reform propositions have simply exacerbated the dilemmas generated by traditional, mass production schooling. As we have seen in the last chapter, the main issues are that:

- Inequality has grown despite massive increases in education spending and infrastructure; and despite a proportionate growth in absolute numbers participating in qualification-bearing courses at each age and stage.

- Relative performance in tests and examinations, participation in post-compulsory education, and subsequent progress to professional and managerial employment, continue to be strongly influenced by family background, education and status.

- Schools have not overcome the social, cultural and family influences on learning, so that disadvantaged children fail to develop their full potential, as measured in terms of their skills, knowledge and perceived self-efficacy.

- School structures, including the curriculum, teaching methods and hyper-accountability testing, emphasise academic knowledge, individual progress and competition; and discount students' personal experience, interests and relationships.

- Competitive schooling compounds disadvantage so that many young people experience feelings of alienation, personal failure and low self-esteem. Passing or failing examinations seems more important than acquiring useful skills and knowledge or working cooperatively with others.

- Disadvantaged students become marginal within their schools and are gradually excluded from the social, economic and political dimensions of citizenship.

Recovering the Progressive Vision

After a prolonged national campaign, in which every resource of government has been mobilised, there is no evidence that the five effectiveness propositions, individually or in combination, have made a serious impression on inequality or disadvantage. Although governments have been hyperactive, producing wave after wave of legislation and innumerable initiatives, education policy is bereft of new ideas. Alan Milburn (2009) and his Panel on Fair Access to the Professions carefully document the dispiriting evidence on social mobility and disadvantage but their recommendations (more city academies, more careers advice, reforming the gifted and talented programme, more focus on school outcomes, education vouchers) are based on the same individualist, human capital theory solutions that have failed to promote social mobility and eradicate disadvantage.

In these circumstances, the progressive tradition provides a critical perspective on a competitive, self-help philosophy that values people in terms of their functional success as employees and consumers. A national obsession with tests and performance has reduced learning to a set of tricks to be mastered, while the student's desire to explore and question has become an obstacle to effective learning by rote, rather than the foundation for personal growth. The progressive critique, together with the practical experience of the early comprehensives, has the potential, therefore, to inspire alternative approaches to learning and to open new, constructive possibilities for all our children.

There are three main areas where progressive insights can help as we engage with the problem of learning and disadvantage, and seek principles to guide our reconstruction of the education service:

- Community and The Personal Life
- Democracy and Learning
- Democracy and Leadership

Community and The Personal Life

The community college, with its organic conception of people living and learning together, is a direct challenge to the ideology of education markets, where citizens become consumers, asked to choose options from an apparently full menu of quasi-commercial public services. As consumers, people cease to belong to an association where everyone contributes for the common good. Instead, they are expected to operate as self-regarding individuals, bereft of common purposes or goals and defined only by their economic relationships and interests. The market reduces learning from a shared activity and purpose to the private, individual acquisition of skills and expertise.

John Dewey, however, was clear that the common school was the agent of the community, responsible for transmitting cultural and intellectual resources and for enabling young people to participate in the life of the group to which they belonged. He believed schools should prepare students to live harmoniously together, despite their diverse cultural backgrounds. The common school should reconcile cultural differences to avoid the kinds of fragmentation that might destroy the community altogether (Dewey, 1916; Pring, 2007). In his influential book *Equality*, R.H. Tawney argues that a shared sense of common humanity and common needs are a better foundation for a good society than an emphasis on individual status and wealth. Communities should 'stress lightly' inevitable differences in birth, status and wealth, and should establish on firm foundations educational institutions that meet common needs and provide enlightenment and enjoyment for all (Tawney, 1938).

Michael Fielding (2000) believes the Scottish philosopher, John Macmurray, provides an important alternative to competitive individualism by insisting that community is central, and by asserting that humans are by their nature communal beings. Macmurray's (1953) philosophical rationale for community education rejects the assumption that the 'Self is an isolated individual' and argues against a purely functional view of human life and purposes. He suggests instead that a community is a group of individuals, united in a common life and fellowship, who cooperate to achieve a purpose. For Macmurray, community is not about place, time and memory, but is rooted in the reciprocal experience people have as persons in certain relationships – 'it is an experience of being that is alive in its mutuality and vibrant in its sense of possibility' (Fielding, 2000:401).

Economic, functional purposes, he argues, are secondary to the fulfilment of personal life through community. Economic efficiency should not be pursued at the expense of the personal life. Although schools have a clear functional role, in terms of socialising young people and equipping them with useful skills, their primary purpose is personal and educational. Macmurray (1954:159) envisages a 'universal community of persons in which each cares for all the others and no one for himself' where the aim is the full realisation of each person's capacity to act. Short of this ideal, people are possessed with 'suppressed, negative motivation' and there is an all-pervasive and unresolved fear that 'inhibits action and destroys freedom'.

Fielding (2000:409) formulates four fundamental questions that challenge existing educational arrangements and the extent to which they are genuinely person-centred and emancipatory:

1. Is the technical or functional for the sake of the personal, for the sake of community?

2. Is the technical/functional informed by and expressive of the personal?

3. How does the principle of freedom inform the relations between those involved?

4. How does the principle of equality inform the relations between those involved?

These questions expose the shallow, instrumental values of contemporary education and show the futility of expecting an effectiveness regime based on functional, utilitarian goals to transform personal lives and the communities where those lives are lived. School reform discounts the personal, and allows no place for the principles of liberty and equality so important if each individual is to develop his or her capacity to act to the fullest extent.

The policy implications are profound. Such phrases as 'social inclusion', 'social cohesion' and 'social justice' are meaningless if there are no community purposes, no common schools and no common goals. Markets and choice encourage families to seek schools where children can acquire the skills to get ahead, rather than share in activities that contribute to the growth of the community and its culture. Social mobility is promoted as if the most natural and important ambition is to leave parents, family and friends behind, in a ruthless quest for individual status and wealth. Better-off families exploit the education market to improve their position with calculated efficiency, while the disadvantaged are stranded, permanent members of an increasingly impoverished community (Ball, 2003a). Housing developments that increase social divisions together with distorted school intakes produce unbalanced communities that benefit no one.

The progressive critique enables us to understand that government policies often make the problems they are supposed to solve much worse. In the age of globalisation, communities have become fragile and vulnerable – yet we behave as if they were infinitely resilient. Although we know that when a village school dies, something in the community is irretrievably lost, we remain locked into a system of markets and choice that has proved ever more damaging for social cohesion.

Democracy and Learning

Progressive educators (e.g John Dewey, A.S. Neill, Robert Mackenzie, John Watts) never doubted that schools should be open and democratic, with students and teachers encouraged to learn and debate without undue deference to authority and tradition. They rejected completely the idea that education is about absorbing neatly defined packets of knowledge provided by experts, and believed instead that children learn through a social and cooperative process that needs space and freedom. This natural inclination to question received opinions and beliefs also contributes to the diversity and growth of the wider community.

David Held (1987) envisages a 'double democratisation' where education and society develop the conditions for each other's growth, with common schools becoming democratic communities that prepare young people for active citizenship, and with local and extended communities contributing to the rich culture and diversity of the school. In these circumstances, Fielding (2007:545) argues, schools have democratic obligations, both to themselves as communities, and to the wider society. He identifies seven areas to which schools should give attention:

- Their overt democratic coherence
- Their endorsement of a vibrant, inclusive public realm
- Their interpersonal and structural integrity
- Their radical approaches to curriculum and assessment
- Their insistent affirmation of possibility
- Their delight and belief in intergenerational reciprocity
- Their interrogative, dialogic openness.

These concerns are utterly remote from today's hyper-accountability regime based on close supervision, standardised knowledge and intensive testing. As we have seen, students are force-fed what is needed to meet specified performance criteria – the space for independent learning, exploration and creativity has been reduced to the margins by ever-increasing demands for better grades.

The extent to which teachers and children have been harnessed to a remorseless, essentially anti-democratic machine is revealed by reactions to the scrapping of national tests for fourteen year olds. When mandatory testing for Key Stage 3 was ended in 2008, some teachers confessed to *The Guardian* (14 October) that they were lost for what to do with their year 9s – they could think of nothing to replace the routine of working through practice test papers. Sir Ken Robinson, an expert in arts education, is less than surprised. He believes standardised education is 'stifling some of the most important capacities that young people now need to make their way in the increasingly demanding world of the 21st century – the powers of creative thinking'. Robinson is convinced that children start at school with sparkling imaginations, fertile minds and a willingness to take risks with their thinking. Unfortunately the school system ensures that few of them ever get to explore the full range of their abilities and interests. Education, he claims, stifles 'individual talents and abilities' and obliterates the desire and motivation to learn (Shepherd, 2009).

This is entirely consistent with John Dewey's (1897) emphasis on the child's involvement with others, rather than test outcomes, as the centre of learning. He believes that true education begins when children are stimulated by the demands of various social situations. As a result, youngsters emerge from their original narrowness of action and feelings, and conceive of themselves in relation to the group to which they belong. They learn the social meaning of their own activities through other people's responses.

Jerome Bruner reminds us that 'interest in the material to be learned is the best stimulus to learning, rather than such external goals as grades or later competitive advantage'. In an age of increasing spectatorship, 'motives for learning must be kept from going passive... they must be based as much as possible upon the arousal of interest in what there is to be learned, and they must be kept broad and diverse in expression'. Bruner challenges orthodox classroom practice. He argues that the teaching and learning of structure, rather than the mastery of knowledge, facts and techniques, is important for later understanding. Teachers should provide a general picture that helps children connect things encountered earlier and later in their development (1960:14,80).

The standardised, test-driven system is in effect anti-educational, therefore, and creates damaging teacher and student mindsets that limit understanding of the world. Based on handed-down 'facts and techniques', the system deprives children of opportunities to explore and experience the world, and to construct narratives that make sense of their journeys. Bruner (1990) is troubled that the bureaucratic imperative in education silences all except the official story of what is happening. He claims that the impoverishment of narrative resources leads to the breakdown of civilised life, tangible in the urban ghetto and the Palestinian refugee compound.

Policy-makers may consider this an extreme interpretation of the National Curriculum and testing regime but what are we to make of a system that defines the detailed knowledge that children are supposed to learn, and emphasises tests and examinations so there is no time for questions and no space for individual exploration? How should we interpret the neglect of the arts and the disproportionate emphasis on academic knowledge? There is little real doubt that governments have tried to control what is taught and to exclude subjects and methods that may lead to unwelcome conclusions. The neo-liberal narrative has been designed into the philosophical base of the education system since 1988, with a story line that excludes radical and dissenting points of view. Bruner's alternative account provides, therefore, an essential critical insight into the authoritarian, didactic assumptions that inform effective schooling and hyper-accountability.

Democracy and Leadership

Influenced by progressive ideas, many heads and teachers working in comprehensive schools were acutely aware that authority, tradition and didacticism could inhibit or suppress children's natural instincts, including their curiosity and creativity, and so reduce their capacity for learning and citizenship. You do not produce the next generation of active citizens by telling them what to do. You do not build confidence and self-esteem by ensuring that every initiative and instruction is from above or by ceaselessly checking that orders have been carried out to the letter. If you organise children in rows and feed them facts, they are likely to have difficulty in understanding the material because they have not formulated and internalised it themselves.

Many educators who grew up with the Nazi and Soviet dictatorships, and experienced the Second World War, were naturally prepared to experiment with less authoritarian approaches to schools and classrooms. They were living, however, with the lingering shadow of the 'headmaster tradition' of educational leadership. This constructed headship as 'personal, powerful, controlling, moralising and patriarchal' (Grace, 1995:11). According to Grace, the 1960s and 1970s were a period of cultural uncertainty and fluidity when heads, particularly in the new comprehensives, could choose between alternative interpretations of their role.

An individual might decide to become an agent of cultural reproduction, and aim to renew and defend traditional academic standards. When my London comprehensive, Eltham Green, opened in 1956, the headteacher, R.H. Davies, wore a gown and emphasised uniform, prefects and twice-yearly examinations that could lead to movement between sets and streams. So-called 'academic' students were siphoned off from art studios and craft workshops to learn Latin. On the other hand, bright young teachers were allowed to innovate. Students wrote, edited, printed and distributed *Vox*, the school newspaper, without any adult censorship. There were annual sixth form conferences on contemporary themes, where debate was openly encouraged. Many schools since, including the new academies, have emulated this defensive strategy, adopting distinctive blazers and emphasising 'traditional' education and examination results.

An increasing number of comprehensive heads chose to carry this a stage further by becoming agents of cultural interruption. They were prepared to experiment with progressive methods and other innovations, particularly in the curriculum. Rex Tregunna, headteacher of The Sir Frederic Osborn School in Welwyn Garden City (reorganised as a comprehensive in 1968), encouraged informality and new ideas. Integrated studies were introduced for eleven year olds, CSE Mode III became a vehicle for curriculum reform, and there was a great flowering of music, drama and sport. Although Tregunna shifted the timetable from streaming to setting, and allowed experiments with mixed ability classes, he also ensured that the school remained outwardly conventional and respectable (Barker, 1979).

A radical minority became agents of cultural transformation, attempting what Grace (1995:14) calls a 'radical reorientation of the cultural and social purpose of the school'. At Countesthorpe College, Tim McMullen was committed to such a transformation. He encouraged colleagues and students to take responsibility for the college and for their own learning. He refused to play the traditional, authoritative role of headteacher. Appointments and promotions were made by groups of staff after full discussion. The Moot, a regular meeting attended by all staff and run without a chairman or formal agenda, governed much of what happened in the school. John Watts, his successor, endorsed this approach (Fletcher *et al*, 1985). Yet, as we have seen, radical experiments like this provoked extreme reactions, leaving the unfortunate impression that progressive heads were misguided or negligent fools who didn't care about discipline or value. The press, in particular, drew the conclusion that the cultural transformers were dangerously permissive and should be resisted at all costs.

The culture wars of the 1970s left progressive education discredited and bruised but the critique of authoritarian, didactic headship remained influential, especially through the school improvement movement. David Hopkins, for example, opposed traditional staff hierarchies, arguing that 'control, accountability, certainty and predictability' were destructive of uniqueness, creativity and individual autonomy (1984: 10/11). He believed that outcome measures like examinations and tests would reduce the quality of education by encouraging more 'instrumental forms teaching' (Hopkins, 1987:5). The solution was to initiate and implement change at school level, shifting control of curriculum and pedagogy as close as possible to the classroom. School improvement should be owned by the school, not imposed from outside. Hopkins and fellow tutors at the Cambridge Institute of Education put this philosophy into practice through the Improving the Quality of Education for All (IQEA) network, based on forty volunteer schools in East

Anglia, North London and Yorkshire. The aim was to emphasise a collaborative, empowering approach, with tutors providing the challenge to increase the teachers' capacity to handle change (Ainscow *et al*, 1996).

For Hopkins and the IQEA network, however, the main priority was to improve the vitality and quality of teaching so that everyone was motivated and engaged. Wider progressive concerns with the community, and with democratic relationships and structures, were increasingly set aside. Leadership was seldom mentioned, as if improvement initiatives alone could transcend power relations and structures. Heads were supposed to be benevolent and detached, providing time, resources and support but otherwise delegating responsibility to their teachers.

Stripped of their democratic and community relevance, progressive ideas about motivation and personal growth may also be found in business-oriented texts about the learning organisation and the self-directed team. Peter Senge (1990:3), for example, envisages learning as a liberating project where people 'expand their capacity to create the results they truly desire ... and where collective aspiration is set free'. Individual team members embark on a self-reflective journey to clarify what really matters to them, to seek personal mastery, to overcome assumptions that impede learning, to build a shared vision, and to understand and think about the systems to which their own small concerns belong. Self-directed teams grew in number and popularity during the 1990s, and dramatic results were reported, suggesting that wide ranging improvements had been made. Self-directed teams were found to take the initiative, focus on team contributions, concentrate on solutions, cooperate, and continually improve and innovate (Elmuti, 1997).

As we have seen, the NCSL has followed this trend, discounting models that emphasise heroic, solo leaders and encouraging policy-makers and practitioners alike to believe that distributed leadership and collaborative cultures have the power to transform schools and colleges. An NCSL sponsored study of eleven schools in three English LAs identified a developmental sequence of six models of distribution, where leadership is devolved incrementally as capable teachers extend their roles and begin to take the initiative (MacBeath, 2005). The NCSL's leadership recommendations are consistent with the school improvement tradition and are derived from progressive insights into the nature of learning. Their aim is to liberate teachers and support staff from rigid hierarchical structures and to empower them to enhance the experience of their students. Two Cambridge Institute IQEA tutors subsequently became government officials[13] and so ensured a continued progressive influence in high places.

This use of progressive ideas in business and education shows their continued relevance and value in providing a theoretical basis for alternative models of leadership. Contemporary, well-managed corporations are inclined to disavow paternalism and hierarchical control systems, and embrace instead progressive, human relations techniques that increase engagement, motivation and productivity. But modern public and private sector organisations are very far from democratic in their fundamental structure and purpose. They are run by highly paid, technocratic managers who are concerned to maximise performance, output and results, with success measured in terms of bottom line results, cost-efficiency and share price. Their employees may be empowered, but in relation to task performance, not organisational agendas and goals (Symon, 2002). The dilemma of teachers is no different. They are expected to become leaders, but they are in no position to lead, let alone to formulate goals different from the template applied by visiting Ofsted inspectors. Self-managing schools, set up to compete in local education markets, have become semi-detached from their communities as they comply with requirements imposed by government agencies (Bridges and McLaughlin, 1994).

Progressive rhetoric has been deployed, therefore, to sell leadership techniques that are potentially totalitarian. Organisation members are expected to commit themselves to the school and its vision without reservation, and without concern for their own values and beliefs. These are not the conditions in which teachers and students can achieve personal growth or contribute to the development of the community (Symon, 2002; Allix, 2000). Michael Fielding's four questions (see above, p137) are an important test, therefore, of the extent to which organisations are genuinely progressive and contribute to the fulfilment of personal life through the community. We need to recognise and reject styles and techniques that are exploitative in their pursuit of functional goals and contribute little to the growth of students and communities.

Building Multi-Ethnic Communities

Everything is not quite as it seems, however. Schools operate within a system that is increasingly over-centralised and over-bureaucratic, but somehow or other leaders 'retain the self-confidence to hang on to a high degree of flexibility and ... have original thoughts and put them into action' (Dunford, 2009a:19). Although everyone is not equally powerful in influencing decisions and outcomes, policy-makers struggle to control the meaning and implementation of their policy texts, which are subject to a process of 'recontextualisation' at every stage of the process (Apple, 2004). The constant emphasis on competition and results may be a pervasive source of pressure for everyone working in the education system, but many school leaders and teachers continue to give a degree of priority to their communities and to the personal growth and development of their students.

A University of Leicester team visited a sample of multi-ethnic schools and colleges in England on behalf of the NCSL and found that their headteachers were unwaveringly committed to attacking ingrained social inequality, particularly racism and poverty. They were aggressive in communicating their values and worked actively to challenge policy, even when this resulted in stressful tensions. One headteacher commented:

> I think the key quality is being prepared to stand up for what you believe is right in human justice terms ... If you're not committed to that type of belief, I don't believe you can work in any school, but you certainly can't work in this school. (quoted in Walker, 2005:10)

All of the case study schools reported here made creating strong links with the community a high priority and devoted considerable resources to developing and improving the connection. The schools saw it as essential to understand what was happening in the lives of the children and built close contacts with parents. Barriers (language issues, transport options, working patterns) were overcome, with outreach work designed to establish effective relationships. Ethnic minority groups were reported to have retained a more collectivist culture through a strong network of local organisations and self-help groups, and to have responded positively to initiatives by the schools (Dimmock *et al*, 2005).

As we saw earlier (chapter 5), this does not apply exclusively to heads working in ethnically diverse communities. School leaders like Mr. Moore, Mr. Turner and Ms. Thomson often find themselves working against the flow of government policy. Social justice issues can be intrusive and disruptive and have to be dealt with, whatever government agencies say about them. Value conflicts are present in any community and successful leadership inevitably involves perceiving and resolving them, within the limits arising from current conditions (Hodgkinson, 1991). The effectiveness framework tends to mask the extent to which school leaders have built schools and communities that work outside national policy to nurture the personal growth of individual students and their families.

Progressive Principles

The leadership case studies discussed above (and in chapter 5) confirm that despite the dominance of the neo-liberal policy agenda, many serving heads are passionately committed to social justice and adopt a progressive perspective in working with their school communities. They draw upon an eclectic mix of practical and theoretical insights to understand and resolve the difficulties that arise from inequality and disadvantage. Their practice is a guide to the principles that should inform policy-makers as they work to transform education policy.

Influenced by the progressive inheritance, many educational leaders understand that their schools should be at the centre of communities, and should serve all the children from those communities, in so far as that is possible. They see leadership as a moral art and they work to forge inclusive, democratic school communities that emphasise personal growth through active involvement with others. They value all students equally and aim to create the climate and conditions for student-centred learning. Divisive streaming and setting arrangements are reduced to the minimum compatible with meeting different learning needs.

The reform apparatus, with its emphasis on tests, examinations and output, frustrates contemporary progressive leaders who understand that curriculum and pedagogy would be greatly enhanced, were they based on intrinsic rather than extrinsic motivation. Progressives understand that little can be achieved without the strongest possible em-

146

phasis on children's interests, curiosity and creativity, and on building their capacity as independent learners. These leaders encourage and promote a wide range of learning opportunities, including community activities that are shared with older generations, with particular emphasis on performance in art, drama, dance, music and sport.

As the pendulum swings, those with this understanding of progressive principles remain optimistic about students and teachers, but have become accustomed to the idea that for the rest of their professional lives they are destined to work with two sets of books, one for themselves and their students, the other for Ofsted inspectors (Barth, 1990). The final chapter considers whether there is hope of something better and investigates how progressive principles should inform the debate about the future.

8

Transforming School Reform

Fear and Hope

This chapter seeks to explain the survival of the neo-liberal consensus despite the financial storm, and considers the continued appeal of school reform in the face of repeated disappointment. It reflects on the fears and hopes that may constrain or assist efforts to influence education policy. The chapter identifies four strategic problems that require urgent action, and recommends key changes of direction and emphasis that are designed to resolve immediate issues and to help create improved conditions for leading and learning in our schools and colleges.

As we peer into the future, we become increasingly apprehensive about the glittering steel edge, keen as a razor, that forms the lower extremity of the swinging pendulum. We see the sweeping, descending crescent, and anticipate the cuts to come (Poe, 1993). The path of the swing is unexpected, however. Failed bankers are earning bonuses again and public service spending is blamed for our plight. Competitive individualism may have galloped over the brink but smart politicians seem more concerned with the ugliness of the poor.

Although the last twelve years have confirmed the raw incompatibility of markets and fairness, voters seem disposed to give trickle-down economics another chance. Despite the tragic twists of the credit crunch, the neo-liberal narrative seems not to have eased its grip on the transatlantic imagination. The market state continues to use the five school reform propositions to promise worth, merit and progress for everyone, although everywhere there is evidence of increased disadvantage and unrelenting failure.

There are three main reasons for neo-liberalism's resilience through damaging booms and slumps. The market narrative has the simple appeal of a parable or fairy story; political elites are protected from unpleasant economic consequences by their practical and emotional disconnection from ordinary people; and there has been no convincing alternative since socialism was discredited by the collapse of planning in the former Soviet bloc.

During the 1980s, I asked a well-known economics professor, then advising the British government on monetary policy, whether Mrs. Thatcher spoke differently behind the scenes. 'Surely she doesn't rabbit on about housewives and handbags when she's closeted with Cambridge scholars like you?' He gave a wry smile and assured me that Mrs. T. argued in exactly the same way in public and in private. She had a good story and she was sticking with it.

The daughter of a Grantham grocer, she believed in Samuel Smiles' doctrine that 'the spirit of self-help is the root of all genuine growth in the individual' and did all she could to promote the myth of an invisible hand guiding markets to deliver wealth for all (Smiles, 1860:1). Her reinvented, self-improving, self-helping, deregulating story seemed to explain the surface prosperity of the 1980s and 1990s. After the Berlin Wall came down, even leading left-of-centre politicians began to accept that there really was no alternative to free market capitalism.

Paolo Freire (1994:24) describes a 'bruising lesson' at a seminar in the 1950s that helped him understand the distance between the lives of ordinary people and the world of bureaucrats and educators. A labourer was outspoken in demanding that Freire understand the people's existence, including their poverty, language, homes and families. This led him to respect knowledge of living experience and to understand that the task of democratic progressive education includes enabling 'the popular classes to develop their language' (1994:39). Officials and advisers are as remote from classroom reality as Freire was from his labourer, and have as little understanding of what it means to work with children. Their ignorance contributes to their confident authoritarianism.

Stephen Ball's (2008) brilliant, all-embracing attack on education policy provides a different type of lesson. Critical scholars become entangled in an obscure theoretical world as they expose the destructive consequences of neo-liberal ideology, and find themselves in a landscape where hope and possibility are seldom found. Ball's diagnosis of the current policy imbroglio is fundamentally pessimistic in documenting the losses and constraints of modernity. Although he reflects on a 'flexible and fluid' world, where 'identities can be continually remade', his analysis offers little hope of fairness and success for all while global markets, competitive economies and the desire for endless growth power the system. Teachers and children are left naked on a blasted heath of discourse, stripped of their human agency by powerful ideological forces roaming the earth in search of victims. Critical theorists risk confirming the assumption that there is no alternative to neo-liberalism and the present policy regime, and that existing agencies and structures are so powerful they are beyond subversion and change (Barker, 2009b).

Although neo-liberal reflexes are apparent in the immediate political responses to the crisis, the early signs of a paradigm shift can be detected. Phillip Blond believes the financial emergency 'represents a disintegration of the idea of the 'market state' and makes obsolete the political consensus of the last 30 years' (Blond, 2009:1). The rise of the red, community-minded Tories represents, therefore, a threat to orthodox beliefs across the political spectrum. Events encourage doubt about the plausibility of the market narrative and apply unexpected pressure to apparently secure assumptions. This is certainly the case in education, where New Labour policies have begun to implode and where there is an urgent need for a new and better direction.

The progressive principles discussed above (chapter 7) help us to expect and understand the failure of authoritarian government policies that have disregarded local communities, discounted young people's perceptions and needs, and denied the relevance of poverty. Personal growth has been sacrificed to the pursuit of national efficiency, while depth and breadth have been abandoned in a drive for impossible results. Bastard leaders and bastard teachers have been made agents of the state, obliged by ruthless inspection to educate by numbers and to do good by stealth. Twenty years after the 1988 Act, Her Majesty's Chief

Inspector's (HMCI)) verdict on school reform in the UK shows that government policies have failed to achieve their objectives and provides discomfiting evidence that should seriously concern disinterested observers.

Schools with a high proportion of deprived children are 'still more likely to be inadequate'. Significant numbers of previously outstanding or good schools 'were found to be satisfactory or inadequate at inspection in 2008/09' (HMCI, 2009:8). A large number (47%) of schools previously judged satisfactory have 'remained static or declined' (p22). For 20 per cent of the academies inspected, 'raising standards and establishing a settled ethos' are a considerable challenge. Overall, there is a 'stubborn core' of inadequate teaching. Too much teaching fails to 'inspire, challenge and extend children' (p8). As a result, too many young people lack essential skills and knowledge and we are not 'keeping pace' with our competitors (p101).

This inspection evidence has the potential to undermine faith in school reform and to stimulate a search for new ideas. The Chief Inspector confirms that the government's national strategies, for example, have ceased to improve children's literacy and numeracy, despite a substantial investment in these 'one size fits all' solutions. We have discovered, after a prolonged and costly experiment, that there is no magic formula to resolve the endemic problem of low attainment. But employers, much encouraged and amplified by the popular press, complain as vociferously as ever about young people's inability to spell and count. Sir Stuart Rose, executive chairman of Marks and Spencer, believes school leavers are 'not fit for work' because they cannot read, write or do arithmetic. Chris Hyman, chief executive of Serco, the outsourcing company, condemns the education sector because it is failing to produce the sort of graduates that industry needs (Jameson, 2009).

The 24-hour news agenda fastens on remarks like these, fuelling commentators whose columns distribute blame before demanding urgent action to deal with shameful problems. The media help create a climate where there is a high probability that inspection reports that refer to 'weakness' in the teaching of basic subjects will be quoted selectively to justify yet another forlorn initiative (HMCI, 2009). The case of the national strategies illustrates how failure of any kind is more likely to be used to prepare the ground for another instalment of reform than to persuade policy-makers that bureaucratic intervention does not work.

Status, Merit and Worth

The media coverage of many education stories, and the desire to 'blame and shame' that accompanies it, are symptomatic of an emotional undercurrent in our society that helps explain the enduring attraction of school reform. The five propositions and the inevitable policy failures they produce may be easily exposed, but there is little hope of change while politicians and important strands of public opinion remain emotionally committed to their current perceptions. What is the source of this emotion? Why does reform enjoy continued popular support, despite the flaws and illusions documented in earlier chapters? We need to understand the meaning and appeal of the reformed school before we can hope to escape the bureaucratic dead hand that grasps our children and teachers.

School reform touches the aspirations of ordinary people by promising equal access to an effective education, through which everyone may acquire the skills and knowledge needed to transcend the past, and share in unlimited prosperity. Competition between schools and between individuals is supposed to produce enterprising workers who gain higher status by creating new wealth. Families (you, me, our parents) are convinced by the idea that education is an opportunity for self-improvement through hard work, and dream of their sons and daughters leading better lives than their own. Successful baby-boomers were the first in their families to attend university and many achieved higher status than their parents, following in the footsteps of pre-war scholarship boys like Alan North (see p49-54). Many poor immigrants see qualifications in western societies as passports to a better life. We are encouraged to claim responsibility for our success and to accept that when things go wrong, we have no one to blame but ourselves.

No one doubts the intrinsic value of education, personal learning and growth. No one questions the truth that very successful students acquire qualifications that can open access to rewarding careers. The supposed causal links between effective education, increased wealth and social mobility are more tenuous, however. The claim that high quality education systems produce wealth is no more valid than the reverse proposition that prosperous societies can afford to educate their children in better conditions and for a longer period of time. Entrepreneurs do not always excel at exams (e.g Alan Sugar left school at 16; Stuart Rose began life as an administrative assistant after not making it to medical school); and exceptional scholars are often less well paid than their former pupils. During the long recent boom, the fastest growth was in unskilled service occupations.

However this may be, improved status (almost by definition) cannot be available for all, even when students are gifted, well educated and hard working. The volume of higher status occupations depends on economic changes strong enough to produce the decline of industrial manual work or the rise of professional society, rather than on school effectiveness. Growing inequality in the US and UK in the 1980s and 1990s has coincided with a dramatic growth in the numbers in secondary and higher education, suggesting that improved skills and knowledge have been insufficient to offset a broad trend towards reduced opportunities for social mobility. Despite supposed improvements in education, there is less room at the top. In these conditions, self help can work for the few but not the many (Bunting, 2009; Perkin, 1989; Milburn, 2009).

The uncomfortable thought that, for most people, learning may have less economic utility than it seems has not disturbed popular belief in education as an essential route to valuable qualifications, increased social and occupational mobility, and higher status. People's vision is limited to close-up scenes of job, family, and neighbourhood. They are aware of themselves and their own striving but have little sense of the wider society of which they are a part. The more people become aware of ambitions and threats that 'transcend their immediate locales, the more trapped they seem to feel' (Wright Mills, 1970:9). Education appears to place destiny in your own hands and offers the prospect of escape. Reformed schools have assumed, therefore, a central place in modern society, not as centres of the community, not as places where people come together for valuable activities that contribute to personal growth, but as custodians and manufactories of status and merit, as creators of value that is defined in relation to national efficiency in global markets.

For policy-makers and consumers alike, therefore, the reformed, effective school serves important functions. Everyone is given access and opportunity, so the government's enthusiasm for neo-liberal and globalising economic policies is legitimised. National regulation and inspection ensure that status and merit are defined and controlled like chateau-bottled wine, and so reassure consumers about the standing of their chosen schools and the value of the qualifications awarded. Performance tables validate local hierarchies and inform the class strategies adopted to ensure an appropriate status match between students and schools (Levačić and Woods, 2002a; Ball, 2003a).

By increasing school effectiveness, and the volume and quality of test and examination results, New Labour has hoped to include everyone, even the most disadvantaged, in a quest for self-improvement and self-advancement. This inclusive policy aim seems to resolve a fundamental moral dilemma in education: the need to balance two competing forms of virtue. One is determined by merit and is assessed competitively (a liberal democratic value); the other by worth, to which all may aspire (a social democratic value). These are inherent moral forces in open societies and the importance attached to each tends to reflect underlying tensions produced by internal and global competition (Rothblatt, 2009). Comprehensive pioneers experienced an acute form of this dilemma when they struggled to find curriculum models and assessment methods that served the needs of very different groups of students. All students were equal (in terms of worth) but some were more equal than others (in terms of merit).

Since 1997, the solution has been to insist that all students, assisted by 'world class' teaching, can and should demonstrate merit in competitive examinations and progress to new levels of skill, knowledge and achievement. This has eluded the distinction between worth and merit and affirms that everyone can improve their skills and contribute to national efficiency. Chart 4 (overleaf) provides evidence that appears to show continuous progress towards a merit distribution wider and deeper than at any time in British education history. The chart shows the annual increase since 1990 in the percentage of 15 year olds attaining 5A*-C GCSE grades (or equivalent). In 1990 only 34 per cent reached the government's merit threshold; by annual increments of approximately 2 per cent the headline figure has risen to the point where 67 per

155

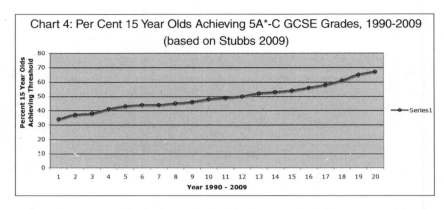

Chart 4: Per Cent 15 Year Olds Achieving 5A*-C GCSE Grades, 1990-2009 (based on Stubbs 2009)

cent of Year 11 students obtain five 'good' GCSE grades and are eligible to study for advanced awards. Should the present trend continue, every school student should attain the threshold by the year 2026.

Evidence of grade inflation (see p10) has led to an annual debate about the validity of these figures. The yearly increase seems remorseless. The trend continues upwards through major changes in subject syllabuses and assessment methods, and never regresses, despite examination board difficulties and recurrent crises in teacher supply. The teaching seems to get better and better and young people's cognitive ability improves beyond all reasonable expectations.

Chart 5 helps explain why critics are unconvinced. The normal distribution or bell curve (black line) is plotted against the 2009 GCSE grade distribution (grey line). As many biological, psychological and social phenomena occur in the population in a distribution known as the bell curve, the black line on the chart represents the result pattern to be

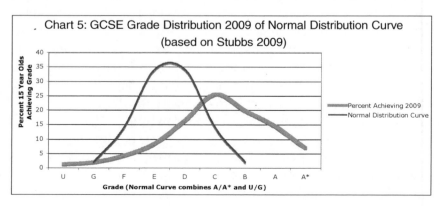

Chart 5: GCSE Grade Distribution 2009 of Normal Distribution Curve (based on Stubbs 2009)

expected in any test or examination. Each year since 1990, the GCSE grade distribution has shifted further and further from this pattern. Few 2009 students obtained lower grades, while there is a strong bias towards the B and C higher grades. Many more students were awarded A and A* grades than U and G grades. This is not a normal distribution and raises many questions about methods that produce better and better grades, despite the known tendency of these types of phenomena to be distributed in a bell pattern. Are the results a function of the methodology rather than the students' attainment? Do the techniques documented by Mansell (2007) produce higher grades from well below average marks?

The government's determination to elude the distinction between merit and worth has culminated in GCSE and A level results so spectacular that they are incredible; and the evidence of grade inflation is so strong that there is a near-catastrophic loss of confidence in the test and examination system. Meanwhile, the clamour from private schools (the exams are too easy) and employers (the students lack basic skills) contributes to a climate of disillusionment and disbelief. Established and aspiring elites fear that their hard won status is threatened by a devalued currency, while the disadvantaged rump on the wrong side of the curve is more disengaged and excluded than ever. The moral dilemma posed by the choice between merit and worth has not gone away.

After the 2008 financial debacle it is obvious to all that the status engine of the school cannot deliver what was promised because it operates in distinctively modern conditions, where inequality has increased and the chances of social mobility are less. People cannot be sure of their jobs and pensions, and fear that their savings may be consumed by the credit crunch. Disappointment is inevitable and exacerbates and intensifies the status anxieties natural to a turbulent environment.

Ordinary people, lacking a sociological imagination and trapped in their own limited orbits, have not responded to this reality by admitting that there are not enough prizes to go round or by recognising that the school system has been annexed to alien economic imperatives that can never be satisfied (Wright Mills, 1970). Despite inevitable disappointment, many parents are unaware that schools are status systems, with a complex pattern of internal niches that reflect the students' social origins. Instead, most believe that schools constitute a neutral learning zone, and provide a source of status and merit, rather than a vehicle for their reproduction and transmission. Driven by insecurity, the reaction is individual and sometimes angry – how do you find the school and neighbourhood that secures a better future? Who should you blame when the desired place does not materialise or when the local school has a bad reputation?

Parents have been taught to compete and to choose, to see education as a self-help project that rewards individual merit and effort. They are insecure and hungry for options that confirm their identities and hopes – not suspecting that their identities will be reproduced and transmitted with the most ordinary help from the school. This is the meaning and appeal of the reformed school – these are the assumptions that keep the neo-liberal experiment alive. Realism about the global reach and emotional pull of school reform should temper the hope that the education apparatus can be easily reformed and that more cooperative models will be welcomed.

Sources of Hope

Ball's (2003b) theoretical pessimism is grounded in the realities of contemporary education, therefore, and is justified in many ways. Bankrupt and misguided policies continue to have traction because they serve the purposes of dominant groups with a disproportionate influence on educational values and practice; teachers are subject to intimidating forms of accountability; and ordinary children are alienated by academic culture and tests that repeatedly expose their perceived inadequacy. But there are pressing, inescapable problems to be resolved, despite these discouraging mega-trends. The government's confused and failing policies have created opportunities for new strategies that may enable teachers and students to find their voices and forge more positive identities. The crisis of faith in the test and examination system is so serious that a new government must listen to constructive proposals for change. Although there is evidence of structural oppression that seems to reduce the space for democracy and personal growth, there are also signs of alternative life, with schools and teachers maintaining humane values and priorities. As the end of term draws closer, there is unexpected room for manoeuvre.

Michael Fielding insists that schools should be a source of optimism and energy in their communities and emphasises their democratic obligation to provide an 'affirmation of possibility' (2007:545). This stress on possibility is consistent with Paolo Freire's claim that without 'a minimum of hope, we cannot so much as start the struggle' and that 'hopelessness can become tragic despair'. Progressive educators, Freire believes, should 'unveil opportunities for hope, no matter what the obstacles may be' (1994:3). His advocacy of hope is far from naïve, however. He contends that the idea of hope transforming the world by itself is an excellent route to hopelessness, and that hope 'demands an anchoring in practice' (1994:2). We need a critical understanding of oppression, but we also need a problem-posing education that is based in participatory dialogue, and is related to people's assertion of their human rights.

Although neo-liberal assumptions persist in Whitehall and Westminster, other sources of hope encourage faith in the possibility of change. At the level of narrative and story telling, school reform has become Frankenstein's monster, criticised by friends as well as by enemies. In a recent address, the Archbishop of Canterbury explained and reflected this important shift of public mood:

> We have in the past few decades created an extraordinarily anxious and in many ways oppressive climate in education at every level in the search for proper accountability ... an inspection regime that is experienced by many teachers as undermining, not supportive, an obsession with testing children from the earliest stages, and in general an atmosphere in most institutions of frantic concern to comply with a multitude of directives – all of this gives a clear message about the priority of tightly measurable achievement over personal or spiritual or emotional concerns. We are in danger of reintroducing by the back door the damaging categorising of children at an early age as successes and failures. This is not a culture that will be turned around overnight – though it is deeply encouraging to see opinion beginning to shift, a shift strongly supported by research like that underpinning the Children's Society's *Good Childhood* document earlier this year... (Williams, 2009:4)

In another development, unnoticed in the world of school reform, the choirmaster, Gareth Malone, has created through BBC television an intensely moving story of alternative educational possibilities, where people and communities are brought together through music and singing to discover sources of self-esteem and happiness. After his success at the Albert Hall, with boys from the Lancaster School in Leicester (see Preface), Gareth was invited to South Oxhey in Hertfordshire, a disadvantaged and 'unsung' town, with no tradition of singing and no community choir. Nine months later, he conducted a mass choir of three hundred adults and children, performing in the open air to the delight of the local community. The four film series ended with Gareth telling the camera:

> We need music, we need music in our communities, we need music in our lives because you need these moments of being together, the whole point of human society is that we come together and we enjoy one another's company and choirs are the culmination of that and an expression of something that is deeply personal and deeply human and you saw that in the choir tonight, the sense they loved singing, they loved it, and so did I, who'd have thought it, South Oxhey absolutely loved singing, it's amazing. (*The Choir: Unsung Town*, BBC 2, September 2009)

Frankenstein's monster can't compete with this. Gareth's story creates hope that personal growth can transcend 'obsessions around productivity, success, busyness' to attain 'a state in which the imagination and the emotions have a proper place' and where the world can be seen as 'both mysterious and capable of change' (Williams, 2009:3-4).

At a practical level, Hal Wallis's production of the film *Casablanca* (see p123) suggests another source of hope. Even in a very tough, top-down regime, talented, creative people succeeded in making a classic by concentrating on practical problems and finding good solutions. There is a clear analogy with schools, where gifted practitioners sometimes seem less constrained by official requirements and instrumental goals than might be expected. Teachers at twelve outstanding schools are reported to work hard to create a culture that 'encourages innovation and experimentation but never allocates blame'. All the schools show a high regard for the 'needs, interests and concerns of each individual student'. At Seven Kings High School, conversations about learning 'happen with all students', with a strong focus on their learning experiences and progress (Ofsted, 2009:15,27).

The principals who build multi-ethnic communities (see p145) have shown a similar ability to work on practical problems, despite the hyper-accountability system. They showed 'they were not passive implementers of policy from above, but were able to shape institutional policies in ways that reflected personal and institutional values' and to seize opportunities presented by new legislation on race relations and children. School leaders proved themselves willing and able to fight for social justice when their schools were threatened by serious challenges (e.g racism) to their integrity and cohesion (Stevenson, 2007a:774-775).

Another source of hope is provided by changes in government policy and rhetoric. Politicians have begun to recognise the self-defeating limitations of school reform and are adjusting themselves to a significant shift in public mood. The accountability regime seemed implacable but in practice has proved unreliable and almost unworkable. As we have seen, testing at Key Stage 3 has been ended, and testing at Key Stage 2 is threatened, with potentially serious consequences. How do you hold schools and teachers accountable without credible data on student progress? There are other important shifts of direction and understanding:

- Ofsted continues to encourage improvement through self-evaluation, although the inspector agenda is derived from a national template and school performance data continues to drive too many judgements.

- Since 2007 the QCA has placed a strong emphasis on customising the National Curriculum to match local needs and circumstances. Schools are asked to provide young people with opportunities to develop social and emotional aspects of learning and to promote thinking skills.

- The NCSL increasingly recommends progressive approaches, including distributed leadership and student voice. Schools are encouraged to collaborate and to accept responsibility for less successful neighbours. There is less emphasis on competition.

- Academy-style freedoms from 'top-down' control are stressed.

- The Prime Minister acknowledges that 'social mobility has not improved in Britain as we would have wanted. A child's social class background at birth is still the best predictor of how well he or she will do at school and later on in life' (Kirkup, 2008).

As politicians manoeuvre on uncertain, shifting terrain, these sources of hope suggest new ways to influence education policy, especially where urgent strategic and practical dilemmas demand attention. *The Pendulum Swings* aims, therefore, to identify realistic priorities for action, based on the arguments and evidence presented in earlier chapters. What is to be done?

Reforming Reform

There is no ideal form for an education system, although officials sometimes give the impression they are working towards a state of republican virtue, where all the levers in the reform signal box are joined up and every train arrives on time. Policy-making is not a neat or rational process and is likely to occur 'at a range of levels almost simultaneously' as 'struggles between opposing values sets' unfold (Bell and Stevenson, 2006:5,23). The current architecture of reform has evolved in unexpected ways, with less logic than protagonists pretend, so the phases of its demise are no easier to fathom than its inception. International comparisons show that although neo-liberal ideology has been pervasive since the 1980s, diverse influences and pressures have produced varied outcomes at different times and places. Few countries have followed the UK's lead, for example, in subjecting schools to intensive scrutiny and regulation. There are less punitive European alternatives (e.g Scandinavia) that outperform us in international league tables and produce apparently more humane, progressive outcomes for their students. These alternatives encourage us to imagine improved arrangements for English education, but the path of events is as yet uncertain (Wrigley, 2005).

The recommendations that follow have been drafted, therefore, in full awareness of the complex and perhaps chaotic influences on policy-making, especially in turbulent times. In these circumstances, my aim is not to launch detailed policy proposals into the confused arena of an election campaign, but to concentrate public attention on four strategic problems that require urgent action. In each case, I seek to demonstrate the threat to the quality of education that has arisen, and to propose changes of style and substance that should contribute to improved conditions for learning. These recommendations do not constitute a progressive master plan, however. Instead, they are designed to help the endless struggle for an education policy that serves the interests of ordinary people.

Strategic Priorities

1 Rebuild Communities

Problem:
Choice and competition have eroded, divided and weakened schools and communities. There has been no compensating benefit.

Progressive Insight:
Education and society need to create the conditions for one another's growth.

As we saw in chapter 7, without personal growth we become obedient automatons, unable to think beyond functional and instrumental goals. Yet our personal growth depends on community relationships and activities that have been devalued and marginalised by the neo-liberal narrative. The fragile social niches contained within the myriad communities of our cities, towns and villages are at risk, threatened like coral reefs by rising water temperatures and toxic chemicals that wash over the delicate organisms within.

New Labour's communitarian policy, initially intended as an inclusive correction to the excesses of Thatcherism (famously associated with the remark 'there is no such thing as society'), is now mainly concerned with isolated individuals and the choices available to them. It has been too weak to compensate for the impact of market forces or to counter the fragmentation produced by new patterns of housing, transport and suburbanisation (Driver and Martell, 1997; Lowe, 1997). National agencies have produced a dependency culture that undermines local initiative, innovation and creativity, without producing compensatory benefits in terms of secure learning gains or targets achieved. Our future depends on rebuilding our communities and restoring their strength and independence as sites of human development.

Phillip Blond recognises that the decline and decay of community has created a political opportunity for the Conservatives and argues that the party should move away from a strong identification with the 'market state' to embrace instead 'a full-blooded 'new localism' which works to empower communities and builds new, vibrant local economies that can uphold the party's civic vision' (Blond, 2009:3). He recommends four priorities:

- Re-localising the banking system
- Developing local capital
- Helping normal people gain new assets
- Breaking up big business monopolies

Blond urges Conservative leader David Cameron to help local communities take ownership of their assets by setting up a new class of local investment trusts, dedicated to investing in the cities and villages they serve. Cameron has the opportunity to be 'a great Conservative premier' if he rejects 'social mobility, meritocracy and the statist and neo-liberal language of opportunity, education and choice' (Blond, 2009:4).

These proposals are a valuable corrective to the vague, nostalgic and often ambiguous ideas that can permeate discussion about schools and communities (Hargreaves, 1982). Blond claims that the 'market state' has reduced many former industrial areas to impoverished ghettoes that degrade the lives of their inhabitants, and argues the priority now is to rebuild local economies and to encourage and support local initiative. We need to be as determined and ingenious in pursuing this new civic emphasis as the 'modernisers' who reduced the powers of local authorities and engineered quasi-markets in the public sector. We should also recognise that a civic mission will have marginal significance while national bodies and agencies take all the important decisions about local services.

There is a danger, however, that communitarians may be dismissed as romantics and utopians, in mourning for the lost social solidarity of pit villages, textile factories and lung disease. This is why the community argument should extend beyond an immediate concern with fixing broken families and deprived neighbourhoods to emphasise that everyone benefits when we come together in common life and fellowship, and that we all lose when we behave as isolated individuals, pursuing selfish and ultimately disappointing ends. Vibrant communities are not band-aids for those at risk of being left behind but groups of individuals who create the conditions for one another's personal growth. Learning is a shared activity and purpose and is diminished when people retreat from one another or when commercial relationships take over.

As advanced societies are inevitably diverse and highly differentiated, there is also considerable scepticism about the possibility of building coherent, organic communities in apparently fragmented urban landscapes. The village communities of pre-industrial England belong to 'the world we have lost' and there is no obvious way to reconcile our desire for a stable status system with our equally important but absurdly contradictory longing for universal social equality (Laslett, 1965). In modern conditions, 'community' seems to depend on an impossibly romantic conception of a defined geographical space where people lead their lives in close proximity with one another. John Macmurray (1953) insists, however, that community is not about place, time or memory. What matters for him is the reciprocal experience people enjoy when they come together in certain relationships. John Dewey (1916) acknowledges the risk of fragmentation but believes common schools should prepare young people to live together, despite the diversity of their ethnic and social backgrounds.

This open definition – of community as an association or fellowship that brings people together in rewarding relationships and contributes to their personal growth – neatly sidesteps unproductive questions about the post-modern condition and directs attention to the altogether more important issue of how to create the conditions where people can gather together and improve the quality of their lives through mutual experiences. This idea frees us from unnecessary reliance on mythical times and places, and helps us to recognise 'community' as an imaginative construct that comprises the multiple associations through which people achieve a life in common with relevant others.

Geographical criteria are not, therefore, essential for successful community building but an equitable distribution of resources between the associations that are formed is of fundamental importance. Policy needs to recognise that it is much more difficult to build strong communities in conditions of acute disadvantage; and that social balance is an important influence on outcomes. We need to do all we can to support local communities and to enable people to find the associations that contribute to their personal growth. Community schools that include students of varied abilities and diverse backgrounds have an important facilitative role to play.

Recommendations

1.1 Adopt a strong communitarian policy to reduce the impact of trends that undermine local communities. Develop firm policy proposals based on Blond's (2009) four priorities.

1.2 Rebalance the roles and responsibilities of national and local bodies. Bring decision-making closer to local communities and encourage agencies working with public services, especially schools, to provide guidance and support rather than control and blame.

1.3 Emphasise the role of schools in building and coordinating community relationships and activity. Ensure that school leaders have defined community responsibilities and that community-building activities are recognised and rewarded.

1.4 Strengthen all schools rather than create new formats that intensify unfair competition. Establish equity between schools (rather than choice) as the main principle informing LA admissions procedures.

1.5 Promote opportunities for local people to participate in art, music, sport, drama and dance. Explore ways to encourage and support community initiatives (e.g the South Oxhey Choir).

---

2 Create the Conditions for Worth, Growth and Achievement

Problem:
The test system overvalues a limited conception of education and rewards slavish attention to mark schemes. Misleading league tables have damaging consequences. Grade inflation has undermined public and user confidence.

Progressive Insight:
Interest in the material to be learned is the best stimulus to learning.

166

The test and examination system that has evolved since 1988 discourages the social, cooperative and dialogic methods conducive to deep and lasting learning. Students are encouraged to anticipate the mark scheme, not to understand and apply an idea. The 'tyranny of testing' (Mansell, 2007) reinforces authority and facilitates the transmission of received ideas and opinions. A narrow conception of education is treated as if it were the only valid currency. Classroom learning and relationships have been hollowed out by test requirements. Seriously unreliable statistical data drives an immensely expensive, time-consuming and destructive system of accountability. Meanwhile, grade inflation has provoked a crisis of public confidence in the standards achieved and the value of the qualifications awarded. There is an urgent need to restore public confidence and establish assessment arrangements that value worth as well as merit.

I do not know the extent to which our politicians and the wider public are prepared for a leap in the dark comparable to that of 1895, when the Revised Code was abandoned. School reform is animated by unacknowledged and deeply emotional status anxieties that may resist continuing evidence of failure, however uncomfortable. The review processes envisaged below create the opportunity to think again about Frankenstein's creature. Do we need this monster? Does he really help our children? What alternatives are possible for children like Debbie and Danièle (see p37-39).

Recommendations:

2.1 Establish a National Commission to (a) recommend renewed educational aims and objectives that reflect a balance between worth, growth and achievement (b) investigate the operation, validity and reliability of the test and examination system (c) recommend assessment practices that recognise and value worth and growth as well as achievement/merit.

2.2 Brief the National Commission to ensure (a) a close match between a broad-based conception of education and the assessment methods used (b) consistency, reliability and validity in national results and standards, in so far as this is possible.

2.3 Restore teacher professionalism through new research-based partnerships between higher education, further education and schools. These partnerships should be entrusted with curriculum design and development within an overall national framework.

---

3 Empower School Leaders and Teachers

Problem:
School leaders and teachers have become bastard managers, expert at complying with external accountability requirements and at every dodge needed to improve results.

Progressive Insight:
Control, accountability, certainty and predictability are destructive of uniqueness, creativity and individual autonomy.

School reform's coercive operational methods are the opposite of those advocated by leading management thinkers, and by the main government body advising on leadership (e.g Deming, 1986; Senge, 1990; NCSL, 2003b). They have predictable consequences, encouraging a system-wide compliance reflex and discouraging independent thought and innovation. A fear-driven, top-down, command and control culture has been created – with professional death penalties for the least successful. Leaders and teachers are bastardised as their goals and targets are set for them. As Hopkins (1984) anticipated, an emphasis on control and accountability has proved destructive of individual autonomy and creativity. Despite all the fear and loathing, however, there is no sign of improved results, once allowance is made for pupils' social background. But we have seen above (chapter 5; also p145/146) that great leaders can transform the qualitative life of their schools – how do we create conditions where their efforts are valued and rewarded?

Dave Allman, a deputy head in Hertfordshire, suggests that a possible solution is firstly, to widen the chosen measures of student progress and secondly, to change the focus of self-evaluation, from the Ofsted template to the school's own agenda. He writes:

> Our problem and the system's problem ... is the maintenance of summative judgments at the end of primary and secondary in terms of quantitative outputs which are used then to reduce hugely complex social phenomena into

what amounts to one single digit, the overall effectiveness of the school on a scale from 1-4.

Ofsted pronounce judgments about the quality of schools employing a particularly harsh system of categorisation. If the numerical grades were to be removed and inspection reports were replaced by wholly qualitative commentary then the playing field would at once become more level. As it stands, Ofsted validates winners at the expense of all others who are terrorised. (Allman, letter to the author, 18.11.2009)

The NCSL models, confirmed by the school case studies discussed in chapter 5, help us understand why authoritarian, top-down leadership styles are unsuccessful and represent a marked advance on the 1960s and 1970s, when many thoughtful heads struggled to reconcile their official status and power with progressive educational goals. The NCSL helps school leaders understand how to promote climates where colleagues feel there is scope for flexibility and initiative; where responsibility and risk-taking are encouraged; where there is clarity about goals and expectations; and where people give extra effort in working towards common objectives. The progressive pioneers, acutely aware that authority and didacticism can suppress the creative spirit, were inclined to underestimate the practical importance of leadership, and sometimes failed to ensure the successful management and coordination of their communities. We have learned since that people do their best in particular conditions and that these should not be left to chance.

The essential problem with positive leadership models of all kinds is that they contain the potential for tyranny, as progressives like McMullen and Neill well understood. Even Senge's (1990:3) vision of liberated but disciplined employees creating 'the results they truly desire' ends with submission to the corporate bottom line. The DCSF believes that the NCSL models should be used to increase productivity – teachers are invited to do their best but only in relation to goals that are imposed from above. This is why the community context discussed above is so important. Leaders should be released from the tyranny of testing but their new responsibility must be for educational arrangements that are genuinely person-centred and emancipatory. Senior teams should become fully accountable to the communities they serve and conduct themselves in ways that enable organisation members to give affirmative answers to Fielding's fundamental questions about freedom and equality (see p137). If they are to succeed with this new responsibility, school leaders will need a broader education in the moral art of leadership than is currently provided (Hodgkinson, 1991; Sergiovanni, 1995).

Recommendations

3.1 Redesign self-evaluation procedures so the school's public accountability is for progress with its own improvement plans, based on a broad conception of learning and achievement.

3.2 Adopt a broad range of qualitative indicators to assess student progress and achievement (see also 2.2).

3.3 Build a broader conception of leadership that recognises professional, moral, and positional sources of authority as well as the purely personal and psychological.

3.4 Establish all schools on Academy terms and conditions but with the local community rather than private individuals as the principal stakeholder.

---

4 Overcome Disadvantage

Problem:
Inequality and disadvantage have increased – inclusion policies have failed to improve outcomes for deprived children. The drive for success (through tests and examinations) has also increased failure.

Progressive Insight:
Schools tend to reproduce and transmit social and cultural characteristics – change is slow and depends on the accumulation of small advantages.

Supposedly 'effective' schools are unable to transform society for reasons that are excluded from official discourse (see chapter 2):

■ 'Effectiveness' relates more to students' family niches (big effect) than to school characteristics (marginal effect), so reflects rather than transforms social conditions.

■ Neo-liberal economic policies have increased inequality and disadvantage – this trend has reduced opportunities for social mobility.

■ The supply of status is not a function of examination results.

■ Niche micro-systems condition student perceptions and expectations, and so constrain upward occupational mobility, even when suitable opportunities are available.

■ Social progress for individuals depends on the accumulation of small advantages. At the right time for certain individuals, education becomes a critical catalyst that converts these advantages into mobility and success. But education does not operate in isolation and does not in itself 'cause' transformation.

■ Mobility and success are important for individuals but have no impact on inequality (as measured by the Gini coefficient) or the disadvantages experienced by those living in the lower reaches of the social pyramid.

■ Competitive tests discourage and marginalise deep learning and personal growth, despite their ability to enrich and sometimes transform people's lives.

Policy-makers, inspired by charismatic advisers like Michael Fullan (2003), have chosen to ignore these painful truths. School reform has converted the education system into a painful treadmill where teachers and students are expected to reverse social history and compensate for an unequal society. Our escape from this *cul-de-sac* is not to be found in classroom science but in understanding that education is intrinsically valuable; and that people's lives can be transformed through shared activities and experiences. There is an urgent need to formulate more realistic goals for individuals and groups – based on personal and community growth rather than on individuals leapfrogging over one another.

Recommendations

4.1 Cease to expect student outcomes that are very different from the social composition of a school intake.

4.2 Recognise that strong communities and schools contribute to the accumulation of small advantages; and that appropriate learning and teaching increase self-esteem and self-efficacy.

4.3 Within the community, insist that employers adopt 'learning organisation' practices to enhance performance, for example by increasing task complexity, control and teamwork.

4.4 Within the school, increase the emphasis on worth and personal growth; and on the student's own interests, creativity and expression.

Transformed?

Schools have been taught to chase shadows and dreams, and as a result have neglected the art of the possible. The South Oxhey Choir shows what can be done, provided we are concerned with personal growth and the community, rather than with status and wealth. Asked by a journalist 'what it is about choirs that is intensely moving', Gareth Malone replied: 'Partly it's this feeling as if the social dream, where everyone comes together and is united, has been realised. It can feel quite Utopian' (Ross, 2008).

Gareth's Utopias, unlike most others, have been brought to life. Interviews with the choir members testified to their joy in coming together to express 'something that is deeply personal and deeply human'. Choir members learned to sing but they also learned about themselves and about one another. In future, nothing will be quite the same again. Gareth's TV projects at Lancaster School and at South Oxhey illustrate how schools should work with their communities, aiming to facilitate mutual relationships that develop people and create conditions that build confidence and commitment. This is how schools and teachers can enrich, improve and even transform real lives.

Notes

1 Dr Arnold was appointed head of Rugby School in 1828. He became famous as an eminent Victorian by turning the struggling school round and establishing a model for other public schools, based on a mixture of muscular Christianity and classical scholarship.

2 The US Federal Reserve's decision not to rescue the insolvent investment bankers, Lehman Brothers, triggered the 2008 economic crisis.

3 Classical free market liberalism emphasises individual freedom and aims to reduce state intervention. Neo-liberals (e.g. Keohane and Nye, 1977) envisage an active, even controlling role for the state, and seek to counter the slothful indolence induced by welfare dependency by encouraging commitment and enterprise.

4 Maximilien Robespierre was a ruthless Jacobin politician during the French Revolution. He dominated the Committee of Public Safety and instigated the Reign of Terror that ended only with his arrest and execution in 1794.

5 Bernard Madoff's investment scheme was exposed during the 2008 crisis as fraudulent. Like Charles Ponzi, who became notorious in 1920, Madoff used funds paid by subsequent investors, rather than actual profits earned, to pay those who trusted him with large sums of money.

6 Alan North was interviewed in 2009 as part of the University of Leicester Vice Chancellors Project.

7 The educational histories of the women in the Barker family are told in Barker (2002).

8 The so-called Black Papers were published at regular intervals after 1969 and denounced progressive and comprehensive education as betrayals of traditional values and standards.

9 Grant-Maintained Schools became Foundation Schools after the 1997 Education Act.

10 The names in this case study have been changed to protect the individuals concerned. Details of the school and other relevant circumstances have been adjusted to avoid the identification of participants. The narrative and dialogue that follow are based on my contemporary notes (February 2009).

11 The case studies, with discussion and analysis, were published in the year shown in the table. Full details are provided in the reference list, e.g. Barker, 2009a, for

Norcross. Quotations in the text below are from interviews with case study participants (usually teachers).

12 John Patten, Conservative Secretary of State for Education, was obliged to settle a libel action out of court after he denounced Tim Brighouse, Chief Education Officer of Birmingham, as 'a madman let loose, wandering around the streets, frightening children' (Judd, 1994).

13 David Hopkins, Chief Advisor on School Standards; Geoff Southworth, Deputy Chief Executive, NCSL.

References

Adonis, A (2005) Better schools, better results: why our teenagers are making the grade. Speech at Christ Church University College, 17 August. http://www.dfes.gov.uk/speeches/media/documents/ alevels.doc (July, 2007)

Adonis, A (2008) Full steam ahead for academies. In *The Times*, 8 January http://www.timesonline.co.uk/tol/comment/columnists/guest_contributors/article 3148855 .ece (March 2009)

Ainscow, M, Hopkins, D, Southworth, G and West, M (1996) *Creating the Conditions for School Improvement*. London: David Fulton

Akerlof, G and Shiller, R (2009) *Animal Spirits: how human psychology drives the economy and why it matters for global capitalism*. Princeton, NJ: Princeton

Allen, R (2007) Allocating pupils to their nearest secondary school: the consequences for social and ability stratification. *Urban Studies* 44(4) p751-770

Allix, N (2000) Transformational leadership. *Educational Management and Administration*, 28(1) p7-20

Apple, M (1989) Critical introduction: ideology and the state in educational policy. In R. Dale (ed) *The State and Education Policy*, p1-14. Milton Keynes: Open University Press

Apple, M (2004) Creating difference: neo-liberalism, neo-Conservatism and the politics of educational reform. *Educational Policy* 18(1) p12-44

Argyris, C (1993) *Knowledge for Action. A guide to overcoming barriers to organizational change*. San Francisco: Jossey Bass

Arnold, M (1960) The twice-revised code. In R. Super (ed) *The Complete Prose Works of Matthew Arnold, Vol. II*. Ann Arbor: University of Michigan Press

Arnold, M (2006) *Culture and Anarchy*. Oxford: Oxford University Press (first published 1869)

ASCL (2008) Why is my CVA lower in 2008? http://www.ascl.org.uk/mainwebsite/resources/document/guidance%20%202008%20cva%20score.pdf (April 2009)

Auld, R (1976) *William Tyndale Junior and Infants Schools Public Inquiry: a report to the Inner London Education Authority by Robin Auld QC*. London: ILEA

Baker, M (2008) Can naming and shaming help schools? BBC News. http://news.bbc.co.uk/1/hi/education/7453301.stm. (October 2009)

Ball, S (1999) Labour, learning and the economy: a 'policy sociology' perspective. *Cambridge Journal of Education* 29(2) p195-206

Ball, S (2003a) *Class Strategies and the Education Market: the middle class and social advantage.* London: RoutledgeFalmer

Ball, S (2003b) The teacher's soul and the terrors of performativity. *Journal of Education Policy* 18(2) p215-228

Ball, S (2008) *The Education Debate.* Bristol: Policy Press

Barber, M (1995) Shedding light on the dark side of the moon. In *The Times Educational Supplement Magazine,* 12 May http://www.tes.co.uk/article.aspx?storycode=11139 (March 2009)

Barber, M (2008) *Instruction to Deliver: fighting to transform Britain's public services.* London: Methuen

Barker, B (1979) HRT at SFO. Unpublished paper in the author's possession

Barker, B (1988) The dangers inherent in Baker's bill. In *The Independent,* 14 April

Barker, B (1989) The Managerial Imperative and the Practice of Leadership in Schools. Review article in *Journal of Curriculum Studies* 21(50) p480-482

Barker, B (2002) Education histories, 1885-2000. *History of Education Society Bulletin,* November, 70 p88-100

Barker, B (2003) Transforming Schools: art, science or illusion? Leicester: Unpublished PhD thesis, University of Leicester

Barker, B (2005) Transforming schools: illusion or reality? *School Leadership and Management* 25(2) p99-116

Barker, B (2006) Rethinking leadership and change: a case study in leadership succession and its impact on school transformation. *Cambridge Journal of Education* 36(2) p277-292

Barker, B (2007) The leadership paradox: can school leaders transform student outcomes? *School Effectiveness and School Improvement* 18(1) p21-43

Barker, B (2008) School reform policy in England since 1988: relentless pursuit of the unattainable. *Journal of Education Policy* 23(6) p669-683

Barker, B (2009a) Public service reform in education: why is progress so slow? *Journal of Educational Administration and History* 41(1) p57-72

Barker, B (2009b) Instruction to Deliver: fighting to transform Britain's public services; The Education Debate: policy and politics in the twenty-first century. Review article in *Educational Management Administration and Leadership* 37(2) p298-300

Barker, B (2009c) What next in school reform? *Forum.* 51(1) p93-99

Barnett, C (1986) *The Audit of War: the illusion and reality of Britain as a great nation.* London: Macmillan

Barth, R (1990) *Improving Schools from Within.* San Francisco, CA: Jossey-Bass

Bass, B and Avolio, B (eds) (1994) *Improving Organizational Effectiveness through Transformational Leadership.* Thousand Oaks London: Sage Publications

BBC News (2004) Inequality: facts behind the fiction. 27 February at: http://news.bbc.co.uk/1/hi/programmes/if/3489508.stm (June 2009)

BBC News (2007) Poorest children 'falling behind'. 31 December http://news.bbc.co.uk/1/hi/education/7165855.stm (June 2009)

BBC News (2008) A level results show big divide.14 August http://news.bbc.co.uk/1/hi/education/7560654.stm (November 2009)

BBC News (2009) Fall in UK university students. 29 January http://news.bbc.co.uk/1/hi/education/7859034.stm (March 2009)

Bell, L and Stevenson, H (2006) *Education Policy: process, themes and impact.* London: Routledge

Benn, C and Chitty, C (1996) *Thirty Years On: is comprehensive education alive and well or struggling to survive?* London: David Fulton

Bennett, N, Wise, C, Woods, P and Harvey, J (2003) *Distributed Leadership: full report.* Nottingham: NCSL

Berg, L (1968) *Risinghill: death of a comprehensive school.* Harmondsworth: Penguin Books

Bernstein, B (1970) Education cannot compensate for society. *New Society*, 26 February, 389 p344-347

Bernstein, B (1971) *Class, Codes and Control. Vol. 1. Theoretical Studies Towards a Sociology of Language.* London: Routledge and Kegan Paul

Blair, T (2001) Our schools can only get better if they are distinct. In *The Times*, 14 February

Blanden, J, Gregg, P and Machin, S (2005) *Intergenerational Mobility in Europe and North America.* London: Centre for Economic Performance, London School of Economics

Blond, P (2009) Rise of the red Tories. *Prospect* 155, 28 February. http://www.prospectmagazine.co.uk/2009/02/riseoftheredtories (November 2009)

Blunkett, D (2000) National college for school leadership (Letter to Richard Greenhalgh, with list of tasks and responsibilities). London: DfEE

Bridges, D and McLaughlin, T (eds) (1994) *Education and the Market Place.* London: Falmer Press

Brown, D (2001) The social sources of educational credentialism: status cultures, labor markets, and organizations. *Sociology of Education*, 74, Extra Issue: Current of Thought: Sociology of Education at the Dawn of the 21st Century p19-34

Bruner, J (1960) *The Process of Education.* Cambridge, Mass.: Harvard University Press

Bruner, J (1990) *Acts of Meaning.* Cambridge, Mass.: Harvard University Press

Bunting, M (2009) Again social evils haunt Britain. Do we still have the spirit to thwart them? In *The Guardian*, 15 June

Butler, T, Hamnett, C, Ramsden, M and Webber, R (2007) The best, the worst and the average: secondary school choice and education performance in East London. *Journal of Education Policy* 22(1) p7-29

Cambridge Primary Review (2009) *Children, their World, their Education: final report and recommendations of the Cambridge Primary Review.* R. Alexander (ed), Abingdon: Routledge

Chitty, C (1989) *Towards a New Education System: the victory of the new right?* London: Falmer Press

Clark, T (2009) Inequality: mother of all evils? *The Guardian*, 13 March

Clarke, J and Newman, J (1997) *The Managerial State: power, politics and ideology in the remaking of social welfare.* London: Sage Publications

Collins, R (1981) Crises and declines in credentialing systems. In R. Collins (ed) *Sociology since Mid- Century.* New York: Academic Press p191-215

Connell, W (2002) *The Educational Thought and Influence of Matthew Arnold.* London: Routledge

Cox, C and Dyson, A (eds) (1969) *Black Paper 1: fight for education.* London: Critical Quarterly Society

Creemers, B (1994) The history, value and purpose of school effectiveness studies. In D. Reynolds *et al.* (eds) *Advances in School Effectiveness Research and Practice.* Oxford: Pergamon

Crowther Report (1959) *Fifteen to Eighteen.* London: Central Advisory Council for Education/HMSO

Cutler, T and Waine, B (1997) *Managing the Welfare State.* Oxford: Berg

Davies, M (2009) *Human Scale Education: human scale by design.* Bristol: Human Scale Education

Day, C and Bakioğlu, A (1996) Development and disenchantment in the professional lives of headteachers. In I. Goodson and A. Hargreaves (eds) *Teachers' Professional Lives.* London: Falmer Press p205-227

DCSF (2008) *Achievement and Attainment Tables,* http://www.dcsf.gov.uk/performancetables/schools_08.shtml (November 2009)

Deem, R, Hillyard, S and Reed, M (2007) *Knowledge, Higher Education, and the New Managerialism: the changing management of UK universities.* Oxford: Oxford University Press

Deming, W (1986) *Out of the Crisis.* Cambridge, Mass.: MIT Press

Dennis, K (2009) Through the looking glass. *Leader* 42 p16-19

Derbyshire, J (2009) The NS profile: Phillip Blond. In *NewStatesman* 19 February http://www.newstatesman.com/society/2009/02/red-tory-blond-liberal (November 2009)

Dewey, J (1897) My pedagogic creed. *The School Journal*, 16th January, LIV(3) p77-80

Dewey, J. (1916) *Democracy and Education.* New York, The Freedom Press

DFEE (1998) *Teachers Meeting the Challenge of Change.* London: The Stationery Office

DfES (2001) Patterns of Educational Attainment in the British Coalfields. *Research report* No. 314. London: HMSO

DfES (2003a) Raising Attainment in Schools in Former Coalfield Areas. *Research report* No. 423. Nottingham: DfES

DfES (2003b) *Widening Participation in Higher Education.* DfES/0301/2003. London: DfES Publications

DfES (2004) *Every Child Matters: Change for Children.* http://www.dcsf.gov.uk/every childmatters/about/aims/aims/ (November 2009)

Dimmock, C, Stevenson, H, Bignold, B, Shah, S and Middlewood, D (2005) Part II: School community perspectives and their leadership implications. In NCSL, *Effective Leadership in Multi-Ethnic Schools.* Nottingham: NCSL

Driver, S and Martell, L (1997) New Labour's communitarianisms. *Critical Social Policy* 17 p27-46

Dunford, J (2002) Transforming secondary schools? *Headlines* 40 p6-8

Dunford, J (2007) New dawn or total eclipse. *Leader* 23 p14-15

Dunford, J (2009a) Using their initiatives? *Leader* 39 p18-19

Dunford, J (2009b) Adding real value to education. *Leader* 40 p14-15

Earthy, S (2009) *Social Class and Health Inequalities.* http://www.soc.surrey.ac.uk/ pdfs/teachingresources/soc102%20-%20lecture%2014%20-%20health%20 inequalities%20and%20social%20class.ppt (July 2009)

Eliot, T (1968) *Christianity and Culture.* New York: Harcourt Brace (first published 1920)

Elmuti, D (1997) Self-managed work teams approach: creative management tool or a fad? *Management Decision* 35(3) p233-239

Eltham Green (1963) *Inspection Report.* London: HMI

Fielding, M (2000) Community, philosophy and education policy. *Journal of Education Policy* 15(4) p397-415

Fielding, M (2007) On the necessity of radical state education: democracy and the common school. *Journal of Philosophy of Education* 41(4) p539-557

Fitz, J, Lee, J and Eke, R (2000) *Inspection, Regulation and Governance: the role of school inspection under Labour.* Cardiff: Paper prepared for the British Educational Research Association Conference, Cardiff University, 7-9 September

Fletcher, C, Caron, M and Williams, W (1985) *Schools on Trial.* Milton Keynes: Open University Press

Freire, P (1994) *Pedagogy of Hope: reliving pedagogy of the oppressed.* New York: Continuum Publishing Company.

Fukuyama, F (1992) *The End of History and the Last Man.* New York, NY: Free Press

Fullan, M (2003) *The Moral Imperative of School Leadership*. Thousand Oaks, CA: Corwin Press

Gardner, H (1993) *Multiple Intelligences: the theory in practice*. New York: Basic Books

George, H (2005) *Progress and Poverty*. New York: Cosimo Inc. (first published 1879)

Gewirtz, S (2002) *The Managerial School: post-welfarism and social justice in education*. London: Routledge

Gewirtz, S, Ball, S and Bowe, R (1995) *Markets, Choice and Equity in Education*. Buckingham: Open University Press

Gilbert R and Gilbert, P (1998) *Masculinity Goes To School*. London: Routledge

Gladwell, M (2008) *Outliers: The story of success*. New York: Little, Brown

Godsi, E (2004) *Violence and Society: making sense of madness and badness*. Ross-on-Wye: PCCS Books

Gold, A, Evans, J, Earley, P, Halpin, D and Collarbone, P (2003) Principled principals? Values driven leadership: evidence from ten case studies of 'outstanding' school leaders. *Educational Management and Administration* 31(2) p127-137

Goldstein, H and Spiegelhalter, D (1996) League tables and their limitations: statistical issues in comparisons of institutional performance. *Journal of the Royal Statistical Society*. Series A (Statistics in Society) 159(3) p385-443

Goldstein, H and Thomas, S (1996) Using examination results as indicators of school and college performance. *Journal of the Royal Statistical Society* 159(1) p149-63

Goldstein, H. (2001) Using pupil performance data for judging schools and teachers: scope and limitations. *British Educational Research Journal* 27(4) p433-43

Gove, M (2009) Freedom for all. *Leader* 40 p28-29

Grace, G (1995) *School Leadership*. London: Falmer Press

Grace, G (1998) Realizing the mission: Catholic approaches to school effectiveness. In R. Slee and G. Weiner (with S Tomlinson) (eds) *School Effectiveness for Whom? Challenges to the School Effectiveness and School Improvement Movement* p17-27. London: Falmer Press

Gray, J (2009) We simply do not know! *London Review of Books* 31(22) p13-14, 19 November

Gray, J, Hopkins, D, Reynolds, D, Wilcox, B, Farrell, S and Jesson. D (1999) *Improving Schools: performance and potential*. Buckingham: Open University Press

Gray, J, Jesson, D and Sime, N (1990) Estimating differences in the examination performances of secondary schools in six LEAS: a multi-level approach to school effectiveness. *Oxford Review of Education* 16(2) p137-58

Greenfield, T and Ribbins, P (eds) (1993) *Greenfield on Educational Administration*. London: Routledge

Grek, S (2009) Governing by numbers: the PISA 'effect' in Europe. *Journal of Education Policy* 24(1) p23-37

Hallinger, P and Heck, R (1998) Exploring the principal's contribution to school effectiveness: 1980-1995. *School Effectiveness and School Improvement* 9(2) p157-191

Haque, Z and Bell, J (2001) Evaluating the performances of minority ethnic pupils in secondary schools. *Oxford Review of Education* 27(3) p357-368

Hargreaves, D (1982) *The Challenge for the Comprehensive School.* London: Routledge and Kegan Paul

Harlen, W (2008) Science as a key component of the primary curriculum: a rationale with policy implications. *Perspectives on Education 1 (primary science),* p4-18. http://www.wellcome.ac.uk/perspectives (September 2009)

Held, D (1987) *Models of Democracy.* Cambridge: Polity Press

HMCI (2009) *The Annual Report of Her Majesty's Chief Inspector of Education, Children's Services and Skills 2008/09.* London: The Stationery Office

Hodgkinson, C (1991) *Educational Leadership: the moral art.* Albany: State University of New York Press

Holt, J (1964) *How Children Fail.* New York: Pitman Publishing Company

Holt, M (1996) 'The making of 'Casablanca' and the making of curriculum.' *Journal of Curriculum Studies* 28(3) p241-251

Holt, M (2002a) It's time to start the slow school movement. *Phi Delta Kappan,* December p265-271

Holt, M (2002b) *The nature and purpose of education.* Centre for Ecoliteracy. http://www.ecoliteracy.org/publications/rsl/maurice-holt.html (March 2009)

Hopkins, D (1984) What is school improvement? Staking out the territory. In D. Hopkins and M. Wideen (eds) *Alternative Perspectives on School Improvement.* Lewes: The Falmer Press

Hopkins, D (1987) Improving the quality of schooling. In D. Hopkins (ed) *Improving the Quality of Schooling: lessons from the OECD International School Improvement Project.* Lewes: The Falmer Press

Hopkins, D (2007) *Every School a Great School: realizing the potential of system leadership.* Maidenhead: Open University Press

Hoskins, K (2010) The price of success? The experiences of four senior working class female academics in the UK. Paper submitted for publication

House of Commons (1999) Education and Employment Committee, Fourth Report, The Work of OFSTED, Vol. I, Report and Proceedings of the Committee. London: The Stationery Office

House of Commons Children, Schools and Families Committee Report (2008) *Testing and Assessment: third report of session 2007-08.* London: House of Commons. http://www.publications.parliament.uk/pa/cm200708/cmselect/cmchilsch/cmchilsch.htm (October 2009)

Hoyle, E (1986) *The Politics of School Management.* Sevenoaks: Hodder and Stoughton

Hoyle, E and Wallace, M (2007) Educational reform: An ironic perspective. *Educational Management Administration and Leadership* 35(1) p9-25

Huxley, A (1934) *Beyond the Mexique Bay.* London: Chatto and Windus

Jackson, B and Marsden, D (1986) *Education and the Working Class.* London: Ark (first published 1962)

Jameson, A (2009) School-leavers are not up to the job, claims Sir Stuart Rose. In *The Times,* 24 November http://business.timesonline.co.uk/tol/business/management/article6928861.ece (November 2009)

Jencks, C, Smith, M, Ackland, H, Bane, M, Cohen, D, Grintis, H, Hegus, B and Micholoson, N (1972) *Inequality: a reassessment of the effect of family and schooling in America.* New York: Basic Books

Judd, J (1994) Patten offers education chief a libel settlement. In *The Independent,* 24 May http://www.independent.co.uk/news/patten-offers-education-chief-a-libel-settlement-corrected-1438029.html. (July 2009)

Judkins, M and Rudd, P (2005) *Evaluation of High-Performing Specialist Schools.* Paper presented at the British Educational Research Association Annual Conference, University of Glamorgan, Pontypridd, 15-17 September. Slough, UK: NFER

Keohane, R and Nye, J (1977) *Power and Interdependence: world politics in transition.* Boston: Little, Brown and Company

Kerckoff, A, Fogelman, K, Crook, D and Reeder, D (1996) *Going Comprehensive in England and Wales.* London: The Woburn Press

Kirk, J (2007) *Class, Culture and Social Change: on the trail of the working class.* Basingstoke: Palgrave Macmillan

Kirkup, C, Sizmur, J, Sturman, L and Lewis, K (2005) Schools' Use of Data in Teaching and Learning. *Research Report* 671. London: DfES

Kirkup, J (2008) Gordon Brown asks for time to prove he can lead the country. In The *Daily Telegraph,* 9 September http://www.telegraph.co.uk/news/newstopics/politics/labour/2711469/Gordon-Brown-asks-for-time-to-prove-he-can-lead-the-country.html (March 2009)

Lareau, A (2003) *Unequal Childhoods: class, race, and family life.* Berkeley: University of California Press

Lasker, G and Mascie-Taylor, C (1989) Effects of social class differences and social mobility on growth in height, weight and body mass index in a British cohort. *Annals of Human Biology* 16(1) p1-8

Laslett, P (1965) *The World We Have Lost.* London: Methuen

Le Grand, J (2006) *Motivation, Agency, and Public Policy: of knights and knaves, pawns and queens.* Oxford: Oxford University Press

Leithwood, K and Levin, B (2005) Assessing School Leader and Leadership Programme Effects on Pupil Learning. *Research Report* 662. London: DfES

Leithwood, K and Riehl, C (2003) *What We Know About Successful School Leadership.* Philadelphia, PA: Temple University http://www.cepa.gse.rutgers.edu/what weknow.pdf (January 2006)

Leithwood, K, Day, C, Sammons, P, Harris, A and Hopkins, D (2006) *Seven Strong Claims about Successful School Leadership*. Nottingham: NCSL and DfES

Levačić, and Woods, P (2002a) Raising school performance in the league tables (part 1): disentangling the effects of social disadvantage. *British Educational Research Journal* 28(2) p207-26

Levačić, R, and Woods, P (2002b) Raising school performance in the league tables (part 2): barriers to responsiveness in three disadvantaged schools. *British Educational Research Journal* 28(2) p227-47

Limond, D (2005) Michael Duane after Risinghill: rise and fall of an educational celebrity. *Journal of Educational Administration and History* 37(1) p85-94

Litwin, G and Stringer, R (1968) *Motivation and Organizational Climate*. Boston: Division of Research, Graduate School of Business Administration, Harvard University

Lowe, R (1997) *Schooling and Social Change 1964-1990*. London: Routledge

Lupton, R (2004) Understanding local contexts for schooling and their implications for school processes and quality. *BERA Research Intelligence*, November, 89

Luyten, H, Visscher, A and Witziers, B (2005) School effectiveness research: from a review of the criticism to recommendations for further development. *School Effectiveness and School Improvement* 16(3) p249-79

Mabey, C and Ramirez, M (2004) *Developing managers: a European perspective*. London: Chartered Management Institute. http://www.managers.org.uk/euromanage mentdevelopment (April 2006)

MacBeath, J (2005) Leadership as distributed: a matter of practice. *School Leadership and Management* 25(4) p349-366

Macmurray, J (1953) *The Self as Agent*. London: Faber and Faber. http://www.gifford lectures.org/Browse.asp?PubID=TPSAGT&Cover=TRUE (July 2009)

Macmurray, J (1954) *Persons in Relation*. http://www.giffordlectures.org/Browse.asp? PubID=TPPIRE&Cover=TRUE (July 2009)

Madison, L and Allison, C (2004) *Learning-Centred Leadership Project: a study of middle leadership in 21 secondary schools*. Nottingham: NCSL. http://www.standards. dfes.gov.uk/ntrp/lib/pdf/Patrick.pdf (January 2006)

Mansell, W (2007) *Education by Numbers: the tyranny of testing*. London: Politico's Publishing

Matthews, P (2009) *How Do School Leaders Successfully Lead Learning?* NCSL: Nottingham. http://www.nationalcollege.org.uk/docinfo?id=23637&filename=how-do-school-leaders-successfully-lead-learning.pdf (October 2009)

McMullen, T (1968) Flexibility for a comprehensive school. *Forum* 10(2) p64-67

McNeil, L (2000) *Contradictions of School Reform: educational costs of standardised testing*. New York: Routledge

McNess, E, Broadfoot, P and Osborn, M (2003) Is the effective compromising the affective? *British Educational Research Journal* 29(2) p243-57

McSmith, A (2009) The rise and rise of Cameron's philosopher-king. In *The Independent* 25 November http://www.independent.co.uk/news/people/news/the-rise-and-rise-of-camerons-philosopherking-1826927.html (November 2009)

Milburn, A (2009) *Unleashing Aspiration: final report of the panel on fair access to the professions.* London: Cabinet Office. http://www.cabinetoffice.gov.uk/strategy/work_areas/accessprofessions.aspx (July 2009)

Miliband, D (2002) *Speech. Annual Meeting of the Association for Foundation and Voluntary Aided Schools.* London: DfES

Miller, R, and Rowan, B (2006) Effects of organic management on student achievement. *American Educational Research Journal* 43(2) p219-253

Ministry of Education (1954) *Early Leaving.* London: Ministry of Education

Morris, H (1925) *The Village College. Being a memorandum on the provision of education and social facilities for the countryside, with special reference to Cambridgeshire (Section XIV).* http://www.infed.org/archives/e-texts/morris-m.htm (July 2009)

Morrison, K (2002) *School Leadership and Complexity Theory.* London: Routledge Falmer

Muijs, D, Campbell, J, Kyriakidis, L and Robinson, W (2005) Making the case for differentiated teacher effectiveness: an overview of research in four key areas. *School Effectiveness and School Improvement* 16(1) p51-70

Mulford, W, Silins, H, and Leithwood, K (2004) *Educational Leadership for Organizational Learning and Improved Student Outcomes.* Dordrecht, The Netherlands: Kluwer Academic

Murphy, P (2007) Summerhill's prophet without honour. *Leopard Magazine*, March http://www.leopardmag.co.uk/feats/151/robert-mackenzie-summerhill. (July 2009)

National Statistics On Line (2009) *Health Inequalities.* http://www.statistics.gov.uk/cci/nugget.asp?id=1899 (July 2009)

NCSL (2001) *Leadership Development Framework.* Nottingham: NCSL

NCSL (2003a) *Leadership Programme for Serving Headteachers: participant guide, Day 1, Day 2.* Nottingham: NCSL

NCSL (2003b) *LPSH – Understanding the concepts.* Nottingham: NCSL

NCSL (2007) *What We Know about School Leadership.* Nottingham: NCSL. http://www.nationalcollege.org.uk/docinfo?id=17480&filename=what-we-know-about-school-leadership.pdf (October 2009)

NCSL (2009) *About Personalised Learning.* Nottingham: NCSL. http://www.nationalcollege.org.uk/index/leadershiplibrary/leadingschools/improving-outcomes-for-schools/personalisedlearning/about-personalised-learning.htm (October 2009)

Neill, A (1962) *Summerhill: a radical approach to education.* London: Victor Gollancz (first published in 1960 as Summerhill: a radical approach to child rearing. New York: Hart)

Newman, J (2001) *Modernizing Governance: New Labour, policy and society.* London: Sage

REFERENCES

Ofsted (1998) *The Annual Report of Her Majesty's Chief Inspector of Schools, 1996/97*. London: The Stationery Office

Ofsted (2009) *Twelve Outstanding Secondary Schools: excelling against the odds.* London: Ofsted

Oliver, P, Davis, I and Bentley, I (1981) *Dunroamin: the suburban semi and its enemies.* London: Barrie and Jenkins

Olssen, M (1996) In defense of the welfare state and of publicly provided education. *Journal of Education Policy* 11 p337-362

ONS (2009) *Annual Abstract of Statistics, No. 145*. London: Office of National Statistics

Owen, R (ed. V. Gatrell) (1969) *A New View of Society and Report to the County of Lanark*. Harmondsworth: Penguin Books (first published 1813/14)

Parkinson, J (2006) When exam stress becomes too much. In BBC News, 16th August. http://news.bbc.co.uk/1/hi/education/4791211.stm (November 2009)

Passeron, J (1990) *Reproduction in Education, Society and Culture*. London: Sage

Perkin, H (1989) *The Rise of Professional Society*. London: Routledge.

Peters, T (1989) *Thriving on Chaos*. London: Pan Books

Peters, T and Waterman, R (1995) *In Search of Excellence*. London: Harper and Row (first published 1982)

Poe, E (1993) *Tales of Mystery and Imagination*. London: Dent

Popper, K (1963) *Conjectures and Refutations: the growth of scientific knowledge*. New York: Basic Books

Pring, R (2007) The common school. *Journal of Philosophy of Education* 41(4) p503-522

PwC (2006) *Academies Evaluation: 3rd annual report*. Nottingham: DfES

PwC (2007) *Research Report: the economic benefits of a degree*. London: PwC

PwC (2008) High Performing Specialist Schools: interim evaluation. *Research Report* No. DCSF-RW034. London: DCSF

QCA (2007a) *The New Secondary Curriculum: what has changed and why*. London: QCA. http://curriculum.qcda.gov.uk/key-stages-3-and-4/developing-your-curriculum/what_has_changed_and_why/index.aspx (October 2009)

QCA (2007b) *English: programme of study for key stage 3 and attainment targets*. London: QCA. http://curriculum.qcda.gov.uk/key-stages-3-and-4/subjects/english/keystage3/index.aspx?return=/key-stages-3-and-4/subjects/index.aspx (October 2009)

Radford, M (2006) Researching classrooms: complexity and chaos. *British Educational Research Journal* 32(2) p177-190

Reay, D and de Waal, A (2009) Debate: a ladder to the top. *Cam* (Cambridge Alumni Magazine) 58 p42-45

Robinson, V (2007) School Leadership and Student Outcomes: identifying what works and why. Winmalee, SW: Australian Council for Educational Leaders: (*Monograph* 41, ACEL)

Ross, D (2008) Gareth Malone: note perfect, Interview by D Ross in *The Independent*, 15 March http://www.independent.co.uk/arts-entertainment/music/features/gareth-malone-note-perfect-794188.html (November 2009).

Rothblatt, S (2009) *Education's Abiding Moral Dilemma: merit and worth in the cross-Atlantic democracies, 1800-2006*. Oxford: Symposium Books

Sainsbury, M and Sizmur, S (1998) Level descriptions in the National Curriculum: what kind of criterion referencing is this? *Oxford Review of Education* 24(2) p181-93

Sammons, P, Hillman, J and Mortimore, P (1995) *Key Characteristics of Effective Schools: a review of school effectiveness research*. London: Ofsted/Institute of Education

Sarason, S (1996) *Revisiting 'The Culture of the School and the Problem of Change'*. New York: Teachers College Press. (first published in 1971 as *The Culture of the School and the Problem of Change*. Boston: Allyn and Bacon)

Sayer, A (2005) *The Moral Significance of Class*. Cambridge: Cambridge University Press

Scheerens, J (1989) *Effective Schooling: research, theory and practice*. London: Cassell

Schmidt, T (2007) Samaritans: young people, emotional health and the DEAL resource. *Education and Health* 25(2) p38-39

Senge, P (1990) *The Fifth Discipline: the art and practice of the learning organization*. London: Random House

Sennett, R and Cobb, J (1972) *The Hidden Injuries of Class*. New York: Vintage Books

Sergiovanni, T (1995) *The Principalship*. Boston: Allyn and Bacon.

Shepherd, J (2009) Fertile minds need feeding. In *The Guardian*, 10 February http://www.guardian.co.uk/education/2009/feb/10/teaching-sats (July 2009)

Simon, B (1988) *Bending the Rules*. London: Lawrence and Wishart

Simon, B (1991) *Education and the Social Order 1940-1990*. London: Lawrence and Wishart

Simon, B (1999) Foreword, in Vlaeminke, M. *op. cit*.

Smail, D (2008) *On Deep History and the Brain*. London: University of California Press

Smiles, S (1860) *Self-Help: with illustrations of character and conduct*. London: John Murray

Smithers, A (2007) *Blair's Education: an international perspective*. Buckingham: Centre for Education and Employment Research, University of Buckingham

Stahl, S (1999) Different strokes for different folks? A critique of learning styles. *American Educator* 23(3) p27-31

Stark, M (1998) No slow fixes either: how failing schools in England are being restored to health, in L. Stoll and K. Myers (eds) *No Quick Fixes*. London; Falmer

REFERENCES

Stenhouse, L (1969) Open-minded teaching. *New Society*, 24 July

Stevenson, H (2007a) A case study in leading schools for social justice: when morals and markets collide. *Journal of Educational Administration* 45(6) p769-781.

Stevenson, H. (2007b) Restructuring teachers' work and trade union responses in England: bargaining for change? *American Educational Research Journal* 44(2) p224-251

Stoll, L and Fink, D (1995) *Changing Our Schools: linking school effectiveness and school improvement*. Buckingham: Open University Press

Strand, S (2008) Minority Ethnic Pupils in the Longitudinal Study of Young People in England: extension report on performance in public examinations at age 16. *Research Report RR029*. Institute of Education, University of Warwick: DCSF

Stubbs, B (2009) *Student Performance Analysis: national percentage figures for GCSE grades*. http://www.bstubbs.co.uk/gcse.htm (November 2009)

Swann, Lord (1985) *Education For All: final report of the committee of inquiry into the education of children from ethnic minority groups. Cmnd 9453*. London: HMSO

Symon, G (2002) The 'reality' of rhetoric and the learning organization in the UK. *Human Resource Development International* 5(2) p155-174

Tawney, R (1922) *Secondary Education for All*. London: Allen and Unwin

Tawney, R (1938) *Equality*. London: George Allen and Unwin

Taylor, F (1911) *The Principles of Scientific Management*. New York: Harper

TDA (2009) *Reducing In-school Variation: making effective practice standard practice. Draft guide*. http://www.tda.gov.uk/leaders/isv.aspx (October 2009)

The Reader Online (2009) *Vital vocabulary*. http://thereaderonline.co.uk/2009/04/vital-vocabulary/ (July 2009)

Thrupp, M (1999) *Schools Making a Difference: let's be realistic*. Buckingham-Philadelphia: Open University Press

Twelftree, M (2007) The perfect supplement. *Leader* 21 p25-6

Universities UK (2007) *Policy Briefing – Spending Review 2007: securing the future*. London: Universities UK

Vlaeminke, M (1999) *The English Higher Grade Schools: a lost opportunity*. London: Woburn Press

Walker, A (2005) Part I: Priorities, strategies and challenges. In *NCSL, Effective Leadership in Multi-Ethnic Schools*, Nottingham: NCSL

Watt, J (2008) *Student Leadership and School Improvement: how can school leaders involve students in the school improvement process through developing students as researchers?* NCSL: Nottingham. http://www.nationalcollege.org.uk/docinfo?id=17402&filename=student-leadership-summary.pdf (October 2009)

Weber, M (1964) *The Theory of Social and Economic Organizations*, trans. Henderson, A and Parsons, T. New York: The Free Press (first published 1947)

Weick, K (1988) Educational organizations as loosely coupled systems. In A Westoby (ed) *Culture and Power in Educational Organizations.* Milton Keynes: Open University Press

Wells, H (1961) *Kipps.* London: Fontana Books. (first published 1905)

West, A and Pennell, H (2000) Publishing school examination results in England: incentives and consequences. *Educational Studies* 26(4) p423-36

West, A and Pennell, H (2003) *Underachievement in Schools.* London: Routledge Falmer

West, A, Hind, A and Pennell, H (2004) Schools admissions and 'selection' in comprehensive schools: policy and practice. *Oxford Review of Education* 30(3) p347-369

Wilkinson, R and Pickett, R (2009) *The Spirit Level: why more equal societies almost always do better.* Harmondsworth: Penguin

Williams, R (2009) *Archbishop's Address: Christian Distinctiveness in our Academies,* Keynote Address at Church of England Academy Family Launch Conference, Lambeth Palace, 21 October

Willis, P (1977) *Learning to Labour.* Farnborough: Saxon House

Wilson, A (2009) *Our Times: the age of Elizabeth II.* London: Arrow Books

Wilson, B and Corcoran, T (1988) *Successful Secondary Schools: visions of excellence in American public education.* London: Falmer

Wintour, P and Curtis, P (2008) I will close up to 270 failing schools to improve standards, says minister. In *The Guardian,* 10 June http://www.guardian.co.uk/education/2008/jun/10/schools.newschools (March 2009)

Wragg, T (1997) Who's to blame and who's to shame? *Guardian Education,* 4 February

Wright Mills, C (1970) *The Sociological Imagination.* Harmondsworth: Penguin Books

Wright, N (2001) Leadership, 'bastard leadership' and managerialism: confronting twin paradoxes in the Blair education project. *Educational Management Administration Leadership* 29(3) p275-290

Wrigley, T (2005) Another school is possible: learning from Europe. *Forum* 47(2-3) p223-232

Index